GREAT HEALTHY FOOD
LACTOSE-FREE

LUCY KNOX & SARAH LOWMAN

CARROLL & BROWN PUBLISHERS LIMITED

First published in 2000 in the United Kingdom by:

Carroll & Brown Publishers Limited
20 Lonsdale Road
Queen's Park
London NW6 6RD

Managing Art Editor Adelle Morris
Editors Salima Hirani, Caroline Uzielli
Photographers Richard Kolker, David Murray

A CIP catalogue record for this book is available from the British Library.

ISBN 1–903258–07–3

Reproduced by Colourscan, Singapore
Printed and bound in Italy by LEGO
First edition

Contents

Introduction

I've always loved food and cookery and, at the age of 25 I was a complete foodie – both my personal and professional lives (I was Cookery Editor of *Woman & Home* magazine) were largely about cooking, eating and entertaining. That was when I developed an intolerance to lactose.

Rather than deprive myself of tasty meals, I became determined to learn how to cook delicious dairy-free meals that my family would be happy to eat on a day-to-day basis, and that dinner guests would enjoy, hopefully without even noticing the lack of dairy produce. I rose to this irresistible challenge and set about experimenting with new ingredients and trying out new approaches to all my favourite recipes. A little imagination and effort brought many wonderful rewards. Before long, I had discovered hundreds of new and delicious recipes and adapted my old ones, and I had a whole new dairy-free diet that I could share with my family and friends. The recipes here are the fruits of my efforts which I hope you will enjoy, whether you or a family member is lactose-intolerant.

LACTOSE INTOLERANCE

Before my condition arose, I had always assumed that lactose intolerance was hereditary. This can be true, but in fact, it can also be triggered off at any stage of your life for a variety of reasons. In my case, I was struck down with salmonella poisoning from a bad egg (an occupational hazard!), which then sparked off the intolerance.

Lactose is a white crystalline sugar present in the milk of humans, cows, sheep and goats. Intolerance is caused when there are insufficient amounts of an enzyme called lactase in the small intestine which allows your body to digest lactose efficiently. If lactose is not digested properly, it causes very painful gastric symptoms. The only cure is, initially, to cut out all dairy produce from your diet in order to allow your body to recover fully. The good news is that after a sufficient rest period of about a month or so, many sufferers can once again enjoy a limited amount of dairy produce. Doctors advise a slow reintroduction of lactose into the diet, starting with those foods which contain low levels of lactose, such as breads, cereals, fermented yogurt and hard cheeses. Some people find that after this initial rest period and gradual reintroduction of such foods, their bodies are even able to cope with a little bit of milk.

Recent research shows that it is far better to reintroduce dairy produce slowly into the diet than to eliminate it for good, which risks the development of other problems caused by a low calcium intake. Nevertheless, your body may never tolerate the levels of dairy foods that it once did. Therefore, it is necessary – and vital to your health – to keep to a predominantly lactose-free diet, so this book should be helpful for many years to come!

FOODS TO EAT FREELY

Build your diet around the following items:

All fresh vegetables – especially green vegetables which contain calcium.

All fruits – fresh and dried.

Seafood, poultry and lean meats.

Pasta, potatoes, rice.

Pulses and nuts.

Breads and cereals – ethnic breads, including French, Italian, pitta, rye, bagels, shredded wheat, porridge oats.

Milk-free substitutes – coconut milk, soya and tofu-based cheese, yogurt, milk and margarine.

Soups – broth-based and bouillon

Condiments – including mustard mayonnaise, ketchup, jams and honey.

Cakes – air cakes.

Confectionery – dark chocolate, marshmallows, licorice and fruit candies.

FOODS TO WATCH OUT FOR

Those items not obviously containing lactose:

Baked goods – croissants, breads, muffins, cakes, biscuits, pastry (not filo), doughnuts, crackers.

Sauces often based on butter and milk, such as white sauce and custard.

Soups – many are milk-based.

Processed foods – meats such as salami often contain lactose.

Egg dishes – pancakes and omelettes (often contain cheese).

Miscellaneous – salad dressings, milk chocolate (plain is fine), ice cream.

Medicines, prescriptions and vitamin supplements – often listed as 'sugar' on the packet but thousands contain lactose.

FOODS TO AVOID

Milk – all types, including condensed, evaporated, goat's and sheep's milk and buttermilk.

Butter/margarine – all types.

Cheese – all types, including cream cheese and cottage cheese.

Cream and yogurt – all types.

Milk proteins (on ingredients list) – whey, lactoglobulin, casein, lactalbumin, sodium caseinate.

NUTRITIONAL KNOW HOW

Cutting out dairy produce eliminates the main sources of calcium and vitamin D. It is, therefore, vital to consume other calcium-rich foods as well as the recommended daily allowances of vitamins A, C and D, phosphorus, magnesium and potassium, all of which aid the absorption of calcium. Plenty of exercise along with a generally healthy lifestyle are also beneficial.

Calcium – canned salmon, mackerel and sardines, tofu, prawns, kale, spinach, brussels sprouts and broccoli.

Vitamin A – carrots, spinach, beans, broccoli, sweet potatoes, peaches and dried apricots.

Vitamin C – citrus fruits, broccoli.

Vitamin D – added to milk products such as margarine, and produced in the body when exposed to sunlight, so unless you spend plenty of time outdoors it may be necessary to take a supplement such as cod liver oil.

Phosphorus – nuts, sardines, eggs, chicken, meat and red beans.

Magnesium – nuts, red and white beans, brewer's yeast and shredded wheat.

Potassium – dried fruits, nuts, avocados, bananas, scallops, chicken, beef and liver.

THE LACTOSE-FREE DIET

As you will see from the recipes in this book, fresh ingredients are the basis of a dairy-free diet. Over the years, I have learned to adapt my shopping and cooking habits to suit a diet that eliminates dairy products. For example, preparing delicious meals with sauces became far easier once I discovered the endless uses of the humble tomato. I now use a variety of simple and tasty tomato-based sauces in place of those based on cream, milk or cheese. Pastry needn't be a problem either, as it can be made easily using oil. Filo pastry, readily available in supermarkets, is a particularly good dairy-free ingredient for both sweet and savoury dishes. Alternatively, a scone-based dough can be used in place of pastry as a substantial topping for pies.

When it comes to desserts, it may at first seem that a lactose-free diet prohibits all the tastiest foods, but this is untrue. Many dairy-free products that are available in health food shops and supermarkets provide delicious alternatives. You can also find ways of cheating;

passing up ice cream became very easy for me once I discovered that I could make equally delicious (and healthier) non-dairy ice cream using coconut milk or oat drink, for example. Lactose-free iced desserts and yogurts are also readily available, taste wonderful and are a lot less fattening than their dairy counterparts.

Dairy products are often added to many ready-made products, so when shopping for your ingredients, make sure you check the labels carefully. If the goods are sold unpackaged don't be afraid to ask the staff for assistance. Bread is a particularly easy product to slip up on, because some bakers use a mixture of milk and water. However, if finding dairy-free bread becomes a problem, why not try making your own bread – the last chapter of this book contains three excellent recipes.

FOR THE KIDS

Unfortunately, many lactose-intolerant sufferers are very young, so I have devoted Chapter 5 to children's meals. Knowing how difficult they can be about food (I have two young daughters of my own), I have included plenty of tasty dishes, such as Pork & Apple Burgers (see page 88) which are lactose-free, but will not make your child feel that he or she is missing out on normal and fun kids' foods. However, before eliminating dairy produce from your child's diet, it is very important to get a proper diagnosis from a doctor or nutritionist as they will be able to monitor the calcium intake, which is a vital element in the diet of a growing body.

I would like to dedicate this book to my parents, Peter and Gina, and to my very dear friend Sarah Lowman, all of whom nursed me day and night during my salmonella scare, when I thought I was going to die, and when, quite frankly, I was not a pleasant person to know. Sarah also proved to be a great source of inspiration and support when I was looking for delicious ways around my lactose intolerance. I would also like to dedicate this book to my husband, Keith Richmond, for picking up the pieces after my illness.

1

Soups & Starters

FRENCH ONION SOUP WITH SUN-DRIED TOMATO TOPPING

2 tablespoons olive oil

700 g onions, peeled and finely sliced

2 teaspoons sugar

30 g plain flour

400 ml game or beef consommé or vegetable stock (see page 77)

Salt and black pepper to taste

Small French stick, sliced

3 tablespoons sun-dried tomato paste

2 cloves garlic, peeled and finely chopped

Serves 4

This traditional soup is given a unique modern twist by replacing the cheese topping with a crispy toasted topping flavoured with sun-dried tomato paste. To caramelize the onions, use good quality olive oil and a generous pinch of sugar as substitutes for butter.

1 Heat the oil in a large heavy-based pan and add the onions and sugar. Cook over very low heat for 10 minutes until the onions are soft and just beginning to brown. Remove from the heat and stir in the flour.

2 Add enough cold water to the consommé to increase the liquid volume to 900 ml. Gradually add the liquid to the pan, stirring constantly. Return the pan to the heat and bring to a boil. Reduce the heat and simmer for 15 minutes, stirring frequently. Season with salt and black pepper.

3 Toast the bread on one side under a hot grill. Turn over and spread thinly with the sun-dried tomato paste and sprinkle with finely chopped garlic.

4 Ladle the soup into 4 ovenproof bowls. To serve, top each portion with a couple of slices of French bread, tomato paste-side up and place under a preheated hot grill for 2–3 minutes until the bread is lightly toasted.

MIXED BEAN SOUP

2 tablespoons olive oil

2 leeks, medium-sized, chopped

1 red pepper, deseeded and finely chopped

1 stalk lemon grass, bruised and finely chopped

2 cloves garlic, peeled and chopped

900 ml vegetable stock (see page 77)

400 g can each pinto beans and flageolet beans, rinsed and drained

2 tablespoons shredded fresh basil leaves

Salt and black pepper to taste

Red pesto to garnish

Serves 4–6

This delicious and fairly substantial soup is quick to prepare and is not puréed, so you do not need to own a food processor. It is wonderful accompanied with warm crusty bread rolls and garnished with a spoonful of red pesto in the centre of each serving.

1 Heat the oil in a large saucepan and add the finely chopped leeks, red pepper, lemon grass and garlic. Cook over low heat for 10 minutes until all the vegetables are slightly softened, but not browned.

2 Add the vegetable stock, stir well, then slowly bring to a boil over medium heat. Reduce the heat and simmer for approximately 10 minutes until all the vegetables are soft.

3 Add the rinsed and drained pinto and flageolet beans to the pan with the vegetables and continue to simmer for a further 5 minutes.

4 Stir the basil leaves into the soup and season with salt and plenty of black pepper to taste. Divide the soup between 4 serving bowls. Swirl the soup with a spoonful of red pesto on to the top of each portion. Serve with warm crusty bread rolls.

BUTTERNUT SQUASH SOUP

Butternut squash has a brilliant orange colour and subtle flavour that marries wonderfully with aromatic herbs such as coriander. This warming soup (see below) is served with home-made garlic croutons.

1 Heat 3 tablespoons of olive oil in a large saucepan and add the onions and 3 cloves of garlic. Cook over medium heat for 5 minutes until the onions are softened. Add the squash, the sweet potato and the coriander and cook for a further 5 minutes.

2 Add the stock to the pan and bring slowly to a boil. Reduce the heat and simmer for 25 minutes until the squash is softened. Ladle the soup into a food processor (in batches if necessary) and blend until smooth or pass the ingredients through a sieve to purée. Season with salt and black pepper. Reheat the soup and serve with croutons.

3 Cut the bread into cubes. Heat the remaining oil in a frying pan and add the bread. Cook over high heat for 5–10 minutes, turning the bread cubes frequently until crispy on all sides. Place them in a paper bag with the remaining garlic, seal the bag, then shake it vigorously to coat the croutons.

6 tablespoons olive oil

2 onions, medium-sized, peeled and chopped

4 cloves garlic, peeled and finely chopped

900 g butternut squash, peeled and diced

150 g sweet potato, peeled and diced

2 teaspoons ground coriander

1 litre chicken or vegetable stock (see page 77)

Salt and black pepper to taste

4 slices bread, crusts removed

Serves 4

SALMON & SAFFRON RISOTTO

2 tablespoons olive oil

2 shallots, peeled and finely chopped

375 g risotto rice

1 tablespoon saffron strands

1 litre hot vegetable stock (see page 77)

375 g salmon fillet, skinned and boned

Salt and black pepper to taste

3 limes, cut into wedges to serve

Handful of fresh coriander leaves to garnish

Serves 6

Pink salmon and bright saffron bring vivid colour to this dish (see below). When making risotto always use Arborio rice. Add a ladleful of stock and wait for it to be completely absorbed by the rice before adding the next – this results in a smooth and creamy texture.

1 Heat the oil in a medium-sized saucepan and add the shallots. Cook over medium heat for 5 minutes, stirring occasionally until they are softened, but not browned.

2 Add the rice to the pan and stir to coat the rice grains in the oil. Add the saffron and one ladleful of hot stock. Lower the heat and cook gently until the rice has absorbed the stock. Continue adding more stock, a ladle at a time, allowing the rice to absorb the liquid before adding the next ladle. This should take 20 minutes.

3 Cut the salmon into bite-sized pieces and add these to the rice pan with the last ladleful of hot stock. Heat the mixture for 3 minutes until the fish is cooked through. Season with salt and black pepper and serve immediately, garnished with lime wedges and coriander leaves.

LEMON THAI PRAWNS

The fashion for Thai food is extremely fortunate for those of us who suffer from a lactose intolerance as dairy produce plays a very minor part in Thai cuisine.

1 Shell the prawns, leaving on the tails. Cut each prawn along the centre of the curve and remove the long black thread that runs along it. Rinse the prawns under cold running water and pat them dry with a sheet of kitchen towel.

2 Place the lemon rind and juice, spring onions, garlic, coriander, chilli and oil in a mixing bowl and stir until all the ingredients are combined. Season with salt and black pepper to taste. Stir the prawns into this mixture, cover and leave to marinate for at least half an hour.

3 When ready to serve, preheat the grill or light a barbecue. Thread the prawns on to the lemon grass stalks and grill for 4–5 minutes on each side until they become pink, turning and brushing with marinade as necessary.

4 To make the dip, mix the soy sauce with the red chilli and coriander. Place in individual bowls and serve with the skewered prawns. Allow 3 skewers per person.

300 g raw tiger prawns

Grated rind and juice of 1 lemon

2 spring onions, sliced

2 cloves garlic, peeled and sliced

2 tablespoons chopped fresh coriander

1 red chilli, deseeded and finely chopped

120 ml olive oil

Salt and black pepper to taste

6 stalks lemon grass, trimmed and halved

6 tablespoons light soy sauce, 1 small red chilli, deseeded and sliced and 1 tablespoon chopped fresh coriander for the dip

Serves 4

GOLDEN SCALLOPS WITH SPINACH

Plump scallops are marinated in a mixture of exotic flavours, before being pan-fried and served on a bed of spinach.

1 Rinse the scallops under cold running water, drain and pat dry with kitchen towel. Place in a large bowl and set aside.

2 Stir together the orange rind and juice, cardamom pods, balsamic vinegar and 1 tablespoon of olive oil in a separate bowl. Pour this mixture over the scallops and leave to marinate for at least half an hour.

3 Remove the scallops from the marinade using a slotted spoon. Place the remaining oil in a large frying pan and leave over high heat until very hot. Add the scallops to the hot oil and cook them quickly over high heat for roughly 3–4 minutes until golden and crispy on the outside but firm and juicy in the middle.

4 Divide the spinach between 6 plates and arrange the scallops on top. (The spinach does not need to be cooked as the heat from the scallops wilts the leaves.) Drizzle balsamic vinegar around the edge of each plate to serve.

18 fresh scallops, washed

Grated rind and juice of 1 orange

4 green cardamom pods, lightly crushed

1 tablespoon balsamic vinegar, plus 1–2 tablespoons extra for serving

2 tablespoons olive oil

125 g young spinach leaves, trimmed

Serves 6

CHICKEN SATAY

Due to the increasing amount of alternatives to dairy products now available in large supermarkets and health food shops, cooking is far less limiting for those with an intolerance to lactose. This recipe uses soya yogurt, creamed coconut and soya milk for a diary-free version of chicken satay (see left).

FOR THE MARINADE

3 tablespoons plain soya yogurt

2 tablespoons crunchy peanut butter

Grated rind and juice of 1 lemon

2 tablespoons coarsely chopped fresh coriander

FOR THE CHICKEN

4 chicken breasts, skinned and boned, cut into thin strips

2 limes, cut into wedges to serve

Chopped fresh coriander to garnish

FOR THE PEANUT DIP

100 g creamed coconut

3 tablespoons soya milk

4 tablespoons crunchy peanut butter

Serves 4

1   Soak 18 wooden skewers in cold water to prevent them from blackening under the grill. Mix the yogurt, peanut butter, lemon rind and juice in a bowl. Stir in the coriander and chicken breasts. When the chicken is evenly coated in the marinade, cover and chill in the refrigerator for 30 minutes.

2   Preheat the grill to the highest setting. Thread the chicken pieces on to the skewers and arrange them on the grill pan. Cook for 3 minutes until the chicken begins to brown. Turn the skewers over and cook for a further 3 minutes until the chicken is cooked through and evenly browned.

3   To make the peanut dip, gradually work the creamed coconut and soya milk until a smooth paste is formed. Stir in the peanut butter and mix well. Serve the hot chicken satay with lime wedges and the peanut dip. Garnish with a little coriander.

TURKEY SATAY

Replace the skinned and boned chicken breasts with two skinned and boned turkey breasts. Cut them into thin strips and follow the recipe as above.

PHEASANT WRAPPED IN PARMA HAM

Succulent pheasant breasts are wrapped in Parma ham, pan-fried and sliced thinly. They are served with a refreshing mixture of watercress leaves and orange slices.

4 pheasant breasts, skinned and boned

Salt and black pepper to taste

8 sage leaves

4 slices Parma ham

2 tablespoons olive oil

80 g watercress and 2 large oranges to serve

Serves 4

1   Make a small pocket in the side of each pheasant breast using a sharp knife. Season inside each pocket with salt and black pepper and slip in 2 sage leaves. Then gently reseal by pressing the meat back together.

2   Wrap a slice of Parma ham right around each breast. Heat the oil in a large frying pan and add the wrapped pheasant breasts. Cook over medium heat for 8–10 minutes on each side until the ham is crisp and the pheasant is cooked through.

3   Remove from the pan and slice the wrapped breasts thinly. Serve on individual plates with watercress leaves and peeled and sliced oranges.

TOASTED CIABATTA SANDWICHES

1 olive ciabatta loaf

1 tablespoon garlic oil

260 g jar chargrilled red peppers

260 g jar chargrilled aubergines

250 g smoked ham, thinly sliced

1 tablespoon chopped fresh marjoram

Salt and black pepper to taste

Makes 2 sandwiches

Chargrilled peppers and aubergines in ciabatta make a tasty sandwich. For a vegetarian option, use fried mushrooms in place of the ham.

Slice the ciabatta loaf horizontally. Grill the cut sides until toasted. Drizzle garlic oil over the toasted sides and sit the loaf on a board. Place a layer of peppers on the bread, then a layer of aubergines, then one of ham. Season each layer, press on the top half of the loaf and slice into 2 sandwiches.

CHARGRILLING VEGETABLES

Preheat a griddle pan. Brush a little olive oil over thick slices of 1 deseeded red pepper and 1 aubergine. Arrange on the pan and cook for 3 minutes on each side until the vegetables are softened and have griddle marks on each side.

MINI PANCAKES WITH BRESAOLA & ROCKET

125 g self-raising flour

½ teaspoon mustard powder

Pinch of salt

2 tablespoons rolled oats

1 egg, medium-sized, beaten

Approximately 150 ml oat milk

Ready-made chilli sauce, 150 g bresaola or smoked meat, sliced and 50 g rocket leaves to serve

Serves 4–6

The peppery taste of rocket works well with bresaola and a little chilli sauce on these savoury pancakes. For a vegetarian option, replace the meat with thinly sliced baby aubergine that has been browned in a tablespoonful of olive oil.

1 Sift the flour with the mustard powder and salt. Stir in the oats and beat in the egg. Add sufficient oat milk to produce a smooth, thick batter.

2 Lightly grease a griddle or frying pan and place over high heat. Once hot, drop spoonfuls of batter on to the griddle and cook for 2 minutes on each side until golden. Cook the pancakes in batches and wrap in a warmed tea towel to keep warm. Serve with chilli sauce, bresaola and rocket leaves.

ROASTED VEGETABLE TARTS

FOR THE SCONE BASE

175 g self-raising flour

1 teaspoon mustard powder

2 eggs, medium-sized

3 tablespoons olive oil

When I first learned I had a problem digesting dairy produce, I thought 'How can I possibly live without pastry?' But I discovered that a scone base prepared with olive oil or oat milk makes a perfect replacement for pastry in many recipes. Here, it provides a good base for the smoky flavour of roasted vegetables in this colourful starter.

1 Preheat oven to 220°C, gas mark 7. Slice off the tops of the peppers and discard, along with the seeds. Cut the flesh into 2 cm chunks.

2 Place the peppers in a large roasting tin with the onion wedges and halved garlic. Drizzle with olive oil and roast for 30 minutes, turning the vegetables once during cooking. Add the quartered tomatoes and roast for a further 15 minutes.

3 Meanwhile, prepare the scone base. Sift the flour with the mustard powder into a bowl and make a well in the centre. Whisk the eggs with the olive oil and 2 teaspoons of cold water. Place this in the well in the centre of the flour and, using a fork, begin to incorporate the flour into the egg mixture until you have a soft, not sticky dough. Place the dough on a lightly floured surface and roll it out evenly. Divide the pastry into 6 and use to line 7.5 cm individual tartlet tins.

4 Divide the vegetables between the tartlet tins. Season with salt and black pepper and sprinkle liberally with thyme. Bake in the preheated oven for 20 minutes. Serve Roasted Vegetable Tartlets warm with a salad.

FOR THE FILLING

4 peppers, 2 red and 2 yellow, medium-sized, deseeded and chopped

1 large onion, peeled and cut into wedges

2 cloves garlic, peeled and halved

4 tablespoons olive oil

450 g tomatoes, quartered and deseeded

Salt and black pepper to taste

Fresh thyme to garnish

Serves 6

GOLDEN ASPARAGUS WITH LEMON PASTA

350 g asparagus tips, trimmed and halved

4 tablespoons lemon oil

350 g fresh tagliolini pasta

3 tablespoons coarsely chopped fresh tarragon

Salt and black pepper to taste

Serves 6

The best time to buy fresh asparagus is between February and June, although canned asparagus is always an option. Fresh tips should be prepared on the day of purchase. This recipe uses lemon oil which can be made at home – add the grated rind of 1 lemon to 200 ml extra virgin olive oil and leave to infuse for at least 24 hours.

1   Heat a griddle pan over medium heat. Arrange the asparagus tips on the pan and drizzle with 1 tablespoon of lemon oil. Cook for roughly 3 minutes on each side, until golden and just cooked through.

2   Meanwhile, bring a large pan of lightly salted water to a boil. Add the pasta to the pan, return to a boil and cook for 2 minutes (or according to packet instructions). Drain and stir in the tarragon, cooked asparagus and remaining oil. Season with salt and black pepper and serve.

MIXED BEAN SALAD

210 g can each of cannellini beans, red kidney beans and flageolet beans

4 tablespoons olive oil

4 teaspoons lemon juice

3 tablespoons chopped flat-leaf parsley

½ teaspoon caster sugar

Salt and black pepper to taste

Serves 6

This attractive combination of beans is highly nutritious and can be altered to suit your taste by changing the variety of beans used.

1   Rinse and drain the cans of beans. Place them in a mixing bowl and stir to mix them together.

2   To make the dressing, blend together the olive oil, lemon juice, chopped flat-leaf parsley, caster sugar and seasoning using a wire whisk. Make sure the ingredients are thoroughly blended.

3   Stir the dressing into the beans. Serve this salad immediately, or cover tightly and chill in the refrigerator for up to 2 hours.

GRILLED CHICORY

3 tablespoons walnut oil

1 tablespoon sherry vinegar

50 g walnut pieces, coarsely chopped

50 g sunflower seeds

4 heads chicory, halved lengthways

Serves 4

Chicory is delicious when grilled – use either the white or red varieties of chicory for this recipe, or try both for an attractive salad.

1   Preheat the grill to a high setting. To make the dressing, blend the walnut oil, vinegar, walnut pieces and sunflower seeds using a wire whisk.

2   Arrange the chicory halves on the grill rack and drizzle a little dressing over them. Cook until they begin to brown around the edges. Remove from the grill, drizzle with the remaining dressing and serve.

CAESAR SALAD

Traditionally, Caesar Salad consists of greens and Parmesan cheese, which can be substituted with soya cheese for an excellent lactose-free version of this popular salad.

1 Separate the leaves from the lettuce heads, wash them, drain thoroughly and set aside. Crumble the soya cheese into a bowl.

2 Remove the crusts from the bread and discard. Cut the slices into small cubes. Heat the olive oil in a frying pan over medium heat and add the crushed garlic. Cook for 1 minute, then add the cubed bread. Fry the cubes of bread for 8 minutes, stirring frequently, until they are golden on all sides. Remove from the pan and drain the excess oil on a sheet of kitchen towel. Leave to cool.

3 Cook the eggs in a small saucepan of boiling water for 3 minutes until soft-boiled. Remove from the pan and plunge into cold water until cool enough to handle.

4 Shell the eggs and break them into a bowl. Using a wire whisk, gradually whisk in the oil, seasoning, lemon juice and Worcestershire sauce. Stir in the anchovies, if using.

5 Arrange the lettuce leaves and croutons in the bowl with the soya cheese. Pour over the dressing, toss gently and serve immediately.

FOR THE SALAD

2 heads cos lettuce

40 g soya cheese

FOR THE CROUTONS

4 thick slices white bread

4 tablespoons olive oil

3 cloves garlic, peeled and crushed

FOR THE DRESSING

2 eggs, medium-sized

90 ml olive oil

Salt and black pepper to taste

Juice of 1 lemon

1 teaspoon Worcestershire sauce

50 g can anchovies, drained and chopped (optional)

Serves 4

CHICKEN CAESAR SALAD

Sprinkle 2 chicken breasts, skinned and boned, with citrus pepper. Preheat the grill to a high setting and cook the chicken breasts for 5–10 minutes on each side until cooked through and browned on the outside. Cut the chicken into cubes or strips and use in place of the soya cheese in the Caesar Salad, above.

FOCACCIA CROUTONS

Focaccia can be used in place of the white bread in the Caesar Salad, above. Cut 4 slices of focaccia into cubes. Heat 1 teaspoon of chilli oil and 3 tablespoons of olive oil in a frying pan and add the focaccia. Cook over high heat, turning frequently, for roughly 8 minutes until evenly browned.

Remove the focaccia from the pan and place immediately in a paper bag with 2 tablespoons of flat-leafed parsley, chopped. Seal the bag and shake well until each crouton is coated in parsley.

HERB & GARLIC CROUTONS

Either slices of focaccia or white bread can be used to make these herb and garlic croutons. Prepare the croutons as described in step 2 above, and place them in a paper bag with 2 peeled and crushed garlic cloves and 2 tablespoons of dried mixed herbs. Seal and shake the bag until each crouton is coated in the garlic and herbs.

2

Lunches & Suppers

FISH
_____

POULTRY
_____

MEAT
_____

VEGETABLES

Warm Mackerel & Potato Salad

250 g new or small pink fir potatoes, washed and halved

4 hearts little gem lettuce, washed and coarsely shredded

4 smoked and peppered mackerel fillets

4 sticks celery, cut into matchsticks

100 ml light olive oil

Juice of 1 lime

1 teaspoon coarse-grain mustard

1 teaspoon clear honey

2 tablespoons snipped fresh chives

Crusty bread rolls to serve

Serves 6

This nutritious and satisfying salad takes only minutes to prepare, making it the ideal supper for the end of a long and hard day. Fresh sardines or anchovies can be used in place of the mackerel if you wish to vary the flavours.

1 Place the potatoes into a medium-sized saucepan of salted water and bring to a boil. Reduce the heat and simmer for approximately 15 minutes, until tender. Drain and set aside.

2 Meanwhile, arrange the washed and shredded lettuce leaves in a serving bowl. Coarsely flake the fish and add to the lettuce. Then add the celery matchsticks and toss the salad gently.

3 To make the dressing, blend together the olive oil, lime juice, mustard and honey using a wire whisk. (Alternatively, place the ingredients in a jar that has a lid and shake vigorously until the dressing ingredients are well combined.) Pour the dressing over the hot potatoes. Toss the potatoes to coat them thoroughly in the dressing.

4 Spoon the dressed potatoes into the centre of the salad and garnish the dish liberally with snipped chives. Serve warm with crusty bread rolls.

Pan-fried Mackerel with Orange & Rosemary

4 small whole mackerel, cleaned

2 oranges, halved and sliced

8 sprigs fresh rosemary

Salt and black pepper to taste

3 tablespoons olive oil

Green salad and crusty bread rolls to serve

Serves 4

Firm-fleshed mackerel has a delicious savoury taste that works well with many flavours, making this a very versatile fish. Traditionally, pan-fried mackerel is cooked in butter, but olive oil is a healthier and dairy-free alternative. When mixed with the sliced oranges and rosemary, you will find that it is just as tasty, too.

1 Rinse the mackerel and pat dry. Divide the sliced oranges and rosemary sprigs into four portions and place 1 portion inside the cavity of each fish. Season inside the cavities with salt and black pepper.

2 Heat the oil in a large frying pan and arrange the mackerel so that they sit side-by-side inside the pan without overlapping (see right). Cook over medium heat for 3–4 minutes, then turn each fish carefully. Cook the other sides for 4–5 minutes until the flesh flakes easily and the skin is golden brown.

3 Remove the mackerel from the pan and arrange one fish on each serving plate. Drizzle a little of the cooking juices on each mackerel and serve with a green salad and crusty bread rolls.

SMOKED COD WITH BACON

675 g smoked cod fillets, skinned

8 rashers rindless back bacon

50 g non-dairy soft margarine

700 g potatoes (mashed with 60 ml oat milk and 45 ml olive oil)

25 g plain flour

450 ml oat milk

2 tablespoons chopped fresh parsley

Salt and black pepper to taste

Serves 4

I was in a restaurant the first time I experienced the combination of smoked cod and bacon and I was amazed at just how well it works. Since then, this dish has become a firm favourite at home.

1   Cut the cod fillets into 4 equal portions. Wrap 1 rasher of bacon around each piece of cod and dot with 25 g of the margarine. Set the cod on a grill pan and arrange the remaining bacon alongside. Grill under medium heat for 3–5 minutes on each side, until the bacon is fairly crispy and the fish flakes easily.

2   Peel and wash the potatoes, cut them into small, even-sized chunks and place them in a large saucepan of boiling salted water. Return to a boil, reduce the heat and simmer for 10 minutes until the potatoes are soft. Drain, then mash the potatoes in the pan with the oat milk and olive oil until smooth. Cover with the pan lid to keep warm and set aside.

3   Place the remaining sunflower margarine, flour and oat milk into a pan over medium heat. Increase the heat and stir the mixture constantly until it gradually comes to a boil. As it does so, it will become a smooth, thick sauce. Reduce the heat and simmer, still stirring, for 1 minute. Finally whisk in the parsley and season with salt and black pepper.

4   Slowly reheat the mashed potato, if necessary, adding more oat milk if it becomes too dry. Place 1 generous spoonful of hot mashed potato in the centre of each serving plate. Set 1 piece of wrapped cod on top of each spoonful of potato and arrange a rasher of crispy bacon on top of the fish. Spoon a little of the herb sauce around each helping using a small ladle. Serve the remaining sauce separately in a jug.

PLAICE WITH PEPPERS

4 tablespoons olive oil

2 leeks, medium-sized, sliced

2 cloves garlic, peeled and thinly sliced

1 red and 1 yellow pepper, cored, halved and sliced

3 plum tomatoes, skinned and coarsely chopped

Salt and black pepper to taste

4 plaice fillets, skinned

Serves 4

This colourful and simple dish is very easy to prepare. Serve it with warm crusty bread and a steamed green vegetable.

1   Heat 2 tablespoons of oil in a saucepan and add the leeks and garlic. Cook gently for 5 minutes, then add the peppers and continue to cook for a further 5 minutes.

2   Stir in the tomatoes and cook until they have softened and most of the liquid has evaporated. Season with salt and black pepper.

3   Rinse the plaice fillets and pat dry. Heat the remaining oil in a large frying pan over medium heat then add the fish. Cook for 2–3 minutes on each side until just golden and cooked through. Serve the pan-fried plaice on warmed plates, drizzled generously with the sauce.

CRISPY HAKE & MATCHSTICK CHIPS

Hake is a low-fat fish with a white, delicately flavoured meat that tastes great when battered. In this recipe I have used a light coating made from whisked egg whites, cornflour and seasoning as a lactose-free alternative to batter.

1 Cut the hake fillet into 4 pieces. Mix the cornflour, salt and black pepper in a bowl. Coat the fish pieces in the seasoned cornflour and set aside. Lightly whisk the egg whites in a bowl, then dip the floured fish pieces into the whites to coat them evenly.

2 Heat the oil in a large, heavy-based frying pan and add the fish. Cook over medium heat until the batter becomes crisp and golden and the fish is firm and cooked through.

3 Place the chillies, parsley, lemon rind and mayonnaise in a food processor and blend until combined. (Alternatively, crush the dry ingredients with a pestle and mortar and whisk into the mayonnaise.) Serve the hake with Matchstick Chips (see page 84) and the chilli mayonnaise.

500 g hake fillet, skinned

4 tablespoons cornflour

Salt and black pepper to taste

Whites of 2 eggs

2 tablespoons sunflower oil

2 red chillies, deseeded and chopped

1 tablespoon chopped fresh parsley

Grated rind of 1 lemon

150 ml ready-made mayonnaise

500 g Matchstick Chips (see page 84)

Serves 4

POTATO-TOPPED FISH PIE

A mixture of fish can be used in this delicious pie according to availability and also to suit your own taste.

1 Preheat the oven to 190°C, gas mark 5. Place the haddock in a shallow pan and pour in the wine and 100 ml cold water. Add the lemon, parsley stalks and peppercorns. Bring to a boil, then simmer for 10 minutes. Scatter the shelled prawns into the pan and cook for 1–2 minutes until the fish flakes easily and the prawns have turned pink. Drain the fish and reserve the cooking liquid. Skin and flake the fish and set aside.

2 Place the potatoes in a saucepan and cover with cold water. Bring the liquid to a boil, reduce the heat and simmer for 15 minutes until the potatoes are soft. Drain and mash the potatoes with the oil, then stir in the chopped parsley and seasoning.

3 Place the flour in a saucepan and gradually work in the reserved cooking liquid. Set the pan over low heat and stir until the mixtures has thickened. Season, then stir in the flaked fish and chopped eggs. Spoon the mixture into a large ovenproof dish.

4 Rinse and drain the spinach and place in a saucepan. Cook for 2–3 minutes until just wilted, then scatter over the fish mixture. Spoon the potato over the spinach and fork it into peaks. Bake for 15 minutes until piping hot.

500 g haddock fillet

100 ml white wine

2 slices lemon

4 parsley stalks

4 black peppercorns

250 g shelled prawns

1 kg potatoes, peeled and chopped

2 tablespoons olive oil

2 tablespoons chopped fresh parsley

Salt and black pepper to taste

2 tablespoons plain flour

4 eggs, medium-sized, hard-boiled, peeled and coarsely chopped

125 g baby spinach leaves, trimmed

Serves 4

CLASSIC KEDGEREE

This delicious dish, ideal for brunch, is also great for a relaxed supper with friends. Smoked haddock is my choice for this recipe, but as an alternative, try fresh or smoked salmon which are equally tasty.

1   Preheat the oven to 200°C, gas mark 6. Grease a 1.7 litre ovenproof dish with oil. Place the haddock in a frying pan that has a lid and pour in the stock. Bring slowly to a boil. Reduce the heat and simmer covered for 8 minutes until the fish flakes easily. Remove the fish from the stock and allow to cool. Then remove the skin, coarsely flake the fish and set aside.

2   Add the rice with the saffron to a large pan of lightly salted boiling water. Bring back to a boil, then reduce the heat and simmer for 10 minutes, or according to packet instructions. Once cooked, drain the rice if necessary.

3   Spoon a layer of rice into the ovenproof dish. Add a layer of fish, then hard-boiled egg quarters and finally, dot with yogurt. Continue layering until all the ingredients are used up. Season each layer with salt and black pepper. Grease a sheet of kitchen foil with oil to cover the dish. Bake in the oven for 15–20 minutes until piping hot. Garnish with coriander to serve.

Oil for greasing

450 g smoked haddock fillet

300 ml fish stock (see page 77)

225 g long-grain white rice, rinsed

½ teaspoon saffron strands

4 eggs, medium-sized, hard-boiled and quartered

3 tablespoons plain soya yogurt

Salt and black pepper to taste

3 tablespoons chopped fresh coriander to garnish

Serves 4

SALAD NICOISE

There are as many versions of Salad Niçoise (see inset, left) as there are cooks in Provence — some dress it up while others dress it down. Usually it contains tomatoes, lettuce hearts, black olives, hard-boiled eggs and tuna. Some cooks use quail's eggs or add pimentos and artichokes, while others like blanched beans and new potatoes.

1   Wash and drain the salad leaves and set aside. Place the quail's eggs into a small saucepan and cover with cold water. Bring to a boil and simmer for 3 minutes. Drain and cool under running cold water. Shell and halve the eggs and set aside.

2   Wash the potatoes and cut any large ones in half. Cook them in boiling water for 15 minutes until tender, then set aside.

3   Blanch the beans in boiling water for 1 minute. Drain, refresh under cold water and drain again.

4   Place the lettuce on a large, flat serving platter. Arrange the hard-boiled eggs, blanched beans, potatoes, olives and tuna chunks on the lettuce.

5   Place all the dressing ingredients in a bowl and blend well using a wire whisk. Pour the dressing over the salad and toss gently. Garnish with rolled anchovies if using, and serve with Herb Bread Rolls (see page 123).

100 g mixed lettuce leaves, such as frisée, rocket and lamb's lettuce

4 quail's eggs

250 g new potatoes

250 g green beans, trimmed

16 black olives

400 g can tuna chunks, drained

Rolled anchovies to garnish (optional)

FOR THE DRESSING

5 tablespoons olive oil

2 tablespoons white wine vinegar

¼ teaspoon wholegrain mustard

1 tablespoon chopped fresh parsley

Salt and black pepper to taste

Serves 2

HERB-COATED TURKEY

Turkey with breadcrumbs is a firm favourite in my family. For extra special results, take the time to marinate the turkey before coating it. Chicken breasts can substitute for turkey, but as these are smaller, use double the quantity.

FOR THE MARINADE

Grated rind and juice of 1 lemon

1 red chilli, deseeded and chopped

2.5 cm root ginger, peeled and sliced

Salt and black pepper to taste

2 turkey breasts, skinned and boned

FOR THE TURKEY & COATING

225 g fresh white breadcrumbs

15 g chopped fresh herbs, such as parsley, oregano and thyme

1 egg, medium-sized, beaten

4 tablespoons clear honey

Serves 4

1 Mix together the lemon rind and juice, chilli, ginger, salt and black pepper in a shallow dish. Cut the turkey breasts in half and add to the dish. Stir the mixture to coat the turkey in the marinade, then cover and leave to stand for at least 1 hour, turning occasionally.

2 Mix the breadcrumbs and herbs together on a plate and season with salt and black pepper, if desired. Press each of the turkey pieces first into the beaten egg, then into the breadcrumbs so that both sides of the pieces are evenly coated in the batter.

3 Arrange the turkey pieces on a grill pan or barbecue. Drizzle with half of the honey and cook over medium heat for 10–15 minutes until golden. Turn each piece over, drizzle with the remaining honey and cook for a further 10–15 minutes until cooked through. Serve immediately with Seared New Potatoes (see page 65) and a simple green salad.

TOPPED BRUSCHETTA

The Italians originally developed this excellent way of making crisp and crunchy toast – sliced fresh bread is lightly brushed with oil that has been mixed with crushed garlic, then baked until crisp in a medium-hot oven. I like to make mine with a mix of olive and walnut oils. The toast stays crisp for roughly 12 hours, so this is the ideal dish for picnics – you can add the toppings when you get there. Serve the bruschetta with Mixed Bean Salad (see page 18).

FOR THE BRUSCHETTA

4 slices French bread

2 tablespoons olive oil

2 tablespoons walnut oil

1–2 cloves garlic, peeled and crushed (optional)

FOR THE ROASTED VEGETABLE TOPPING

100 g chargrilled artichokes in oil, drained and halved

100 g chargrilled mixed peppers in oil, drained and sliced into strips

Fresh basil to garnish

Black pepper to taste

2 tablespoons olive oil for drizzling

1 Preheat the oven to 200°C, gas mark 6. Arrange the slices of French bread side-by-side in a single layer in a large roasting tin.

2 Mix together the olive and walnut oils with the crushed garlic, if using. Brush half of the mixture on to one side of the bread slices. Bake the bread in the preheated oven for 8–10 minutes until crisp and golden, then turn the bread slices over and brush with the remaining oil. Bake for a further 8–10 minutes. Remove the bruschetta from the oven and allow to cool.

3 For the roasted vegetable topping, arrange the strips of chargrilled peppers and the chargrilled artichoke halves on 2 slices of bruschetta. Garnish with basil and sprinkle with black pepper, then drizzle with olive oil directly before serving.

4 For the duck topping, arrange the sliced duck and tomatoes on top of the 2 remaining slices of bruschetta and garnish with thyme or rocket. Drizzle with olive oil and season with black pepper to serve.

PIMENTO AND PESTO PASTES

Either of these pastes may be spread on to slices of French bread in place of the walnut and olive oils and garlic mixture before being baked in the oven. Roasted vegetables are ideal as a topping for either pimento or pesto paste and the duck is particularly tasty with the pimento paste.

To prepare pimento paste, blend the contents of a 160 g can of pimentos with 3 tablespoons of olive oil in a food processor. (Alternatively, crush the pimentos in a mortar with a pestle and mix in the oil.)

For pesto paste, blend 25 g pine nuts and 25 g fresh basil leaves with 6 tablespoons of extra virgin olive oil in a food processor. (Alternatively, crush the pine nuts and basil in a mortar with a pestle and gradually mix in the oil.) Season with salt and black pepper.

FOR THE DUCK TOPPING

1 smoked duck breast, skinned and thinly sliced

4 red cherry tomatoes, halved

4 yellow cherry tomatoes, halved

Fresh thyme or rocket to garnish

2 tablespoons olive oil

Salt and black pepper to taste

Serves 4

CRUNCHY CHICKEN SALAD

This light and tempting meal is my lactose-free version of the old favourite, Coronation chicken.

1 Heat the oil in a frying pan and add the onion. Cook over high heat until softened and beginning to colour. Add the chicken and continue to cook over high heat for 10 minutes on each side until the chicken is golden and cooked through. Remove the chicken from the pan and allow to cool a little, then cut into fine strips and set aside.

2 Meanwhile, stir the curry paste and mango chutney into the pan with the onions. Cook gently for 5 minutes. Remove from the heat and allow to cool.

3 Mix together the peaches, celery, cooled curry mixture and mayonnaise, then stir in the chicken. Cover and chill for at least 30 minutes until ready to serve. Serve with Summer Flower Salad (see below).

2 tablespoons olive oil

1 onion, peeled and chopped

4 chicken breasts, skinned and boned

2 tablespoons mild curry paste

2 tablespoons mango chutney

2 peaches, stoned and cut into matchsticks

1 head celery, rinsed and cut into matchsticks

150 ml mayonnaise

Serves 6

SUMMER FLOWER SALAD

Mix 50 g edible flowers (such as nasturtiums, rose petals, borage or lavender) with 100 g salad leaves (lamb's lettuce, rocket, frisée) and some fresh herbs (flat-leaf parsley, chervil, sage). Dress lightly with an oil and vinegar dressing.

CHICKEN-STUFFED PITTAS

Originally from around Greece and the Middle East, flat, oval pitta breads are traditionally slit open and stuffed. Here, they are given a fruity curried chicken filling.

1 Grill the chicken breasts under a hot grill for 5–10 minutes on each side until cooked through. Leave to cool, then cut into cubes. Warm the pitta breads either in a moderate oven or under a medium-hot grill, then cut along half the circumference of each pitta to open them out into 'pockets'.

2 Mix the spring onions, the cooked, cubed chicken, the mango and grapes. Beat the mayonnaise in a separate bowl with the curry paste, coriander, salt and pepper. Add the chicken mixture to the curried mayonnaise and stir to ensure all the ingredients are thoroughly coated in the sauce.

3 Coarsely shred the lettuces and arrange inside the four pittas. Spoon the chicken mixture into the pittas and serve.

2 chicken breasts, each weighing 175 g

4 white or wholemeal pitta breads

2 spring onions, trimmed and sliced

1 ripe mango, peeled, stoned and cubed

125 g seedless white grapes, halved

4 tablespoons mayonnaise

1 tablespoon mild curry paste

2 tablespoons chopped fresh coriander

Salt and black pepper to taste

2 little gem lettuces

Serves 4

DUCK AND VEGETARIAN STUFFED PITTAS

Replace the chicken with two duck breasts, fried gently in the fat that exudes from the skin, for 6 minutes on each side. Or use 350 g cubed smoked tofu.

Chinese Style Pork

One factor in favour of sesame oil is that a little of it goes a long way. Another is its delicious nutty flavour which gives this stir-fry its authentic Chinese taste.

2 tablespoons sesame oil

350 g pork fillet, cut into thin strips

100 g sugar snap peas, trimmed

100 g broccoli florets

100 g baby sweetcorn, trimmed and halved

1 red pepper, deseeded and thinly sliced

2 spring onions, sliced

50 g bean sprouts

1 teaspoon arrowroot

150 ml vegetable stock (see page 77)

1 teaspoon light soy sauce

Black pepper to taste

Serves 4

1 Heat the sesame oil in a wok or a large frying pan. Add the pork and stir-fry over high heat for 5 minutes, until the pork begins to brown.

2 Add the sugar snap peas, broccoli, sweetcorn, pepper, spring onions and bean sprouts and continue to stir-fry over high heat for 5–6 minutes, until the vegetables just begin to brown and wilt.

3 Blend together the arrowroot and stock and tip the mixture into the pan, stirring constantly to prevent lumps forming. Once the mixture thickens, remove from the heat and season with light soy sauce and black pepper. Serve with fresh rice noodles or plain boiled rice.

CHINESE STYLE BEEF

Substitute thinly sliced beef fillet for the pork fillet. Stir-fry the beef fillet for 1–3 minutes, add the vegetables and cook as above. Sprinkle liberally with toasted sesame seeds (cooked in a very hot frying pan, shaking constantly until the seeds are golden) and serve with a little grated horseradish.

Spicy Beef

To allow the flavours of the spicy beef fully to develop, it is a good idea to prepare this dish in advance, cover it and leave it to stand for 24 hours. The egg topping can be made at the last minute.

2 tablespoons olive oil

1 large onion, peeled and chopped

2 cloves garlic, peeled and chopped

2 tablespoons mild curry paste

500 g lean minced beef

150 ml red wine

2 tablespoons chopped fresh coriander

25 g flaked almonds

2 eggs, medium-sized

300 ml plain soya yogurt

Salt and black pepper

Serves 4

1 Preheat the oven to 180°C, gas mark 4 (if preparing and cooking on the same day). Heat the oil in a large pan and add the onion and garlic. Cook over medium heat for 5 minutes until the onions are translucent. Stir in the curry paste and minced beef. Increase the heat to high and cook until the beef is browned, stirring occasionally to ensure the mixture does not burn.

2 Add the wine and coriander and cook for a further 2 minutes. Spoon the mixture into an ovenproof dish. At this stage, the mince dish can be covered and left in the refrigerator to stand for 24 hours, if desired.

3 Heat a heavy-based frying pan until hot. Add the flaked almonds and cook over low heat for 1–2 minutes, stirring occasionally until the almonds are browned and toasted. Beat together the eggs and yogurt in a mixing bowl and season with salt and black pepper. Pour the egg mixture over the mince mixture and scatter the almonds on top. Bake in the preheated oven for 30 minutes until the 'custard' topping is set and golden.

SAUSAGE & BEAN CASSEROLE

*There is a wide variety of weird and wonderful sausages available, but
I think one of the spicier varieties, such as the Spanish chorizo, is best
for this rich and warming winter casserole.*

1. Preheat the oven to 200°C, gas mark 6. Place the halved bacon rashers in a flameproof casserole that has a lid and cook gently until the fat begins to run. Increase the heat to a medium setting, add the leeks and cook until they soften. Add the salami and chorizo sausage to the casserole and continue to cook for 5 minutes until they begin to brown.

2. Stir the chopped tomatoes and beans into the casserole with the stock and bring to a boil. Reduce the heat and simmer for 15 minutes. Cover the casserole and cook in the preheated oven for 45 minutes.

3. Remove the casserole from the oven, season with salt and black pepper and stir in the parsley. Serve with jacket potatoes.

400 g streaky bacon rashers, halved

2 leeks, trimmed and sliced

150 g salami, thickly sliced

6 chorizo sausages

800 g canned chopped tomatoes

400 g canned cannellini beans, rinsed

300 ml chicken or vegetable stock
(see page 77)

Salt and black pepper to taste

2 tablespoons chopped flat-leaf parsley

Serves 6

SEARED CALF'S LIVER WITH CRISPY BACON

250 g rindless streaky bacon, chopped

1 tablespoon olive oil

2 onions, peeled and sliced

4 slices calf's liver, trimmed

1 tablespoon chopped fresh parsley

Black pepper to taste

Serves 4

Calf's liver is extremely nutritious, being rich in protein, iron and vitamin A, and it is packed full of flavour. The best way to cook it, in my opinion, is with bacon and plenty of fried onions...delicious!

1   Place the bacon in a frying pan and cook over low heat until the fat begins to run. Increase the heat and fry for 10 minutes until crisp and brown. Remove the bacon from the pan using a slotted spoon and set aside.

2   Add the oil to the pan and, when hot, add the onions. Cook over medium heat until softened but not coloured.

3   Arrange the liver on top of the onions and cook for 3–5 minutes on each side. Ensure you do not overcook the liver as it will become tough.

4   Return the bacon to the pan and mix with the liver and onions until heated through. Sprinkle with parsley and season with black pepper (there is no need to add salt as the bacon is sufficiently salty). Serve immediately with fresh peas and potatoes that have been mashed with olive oil and garlic.

LAMB WITH CRISPY POTATOES

FOR THE POTATOES

2 tablespoons olive oil

500 g new potatoes, scrubbed

Large pinch coarse sea salt

4–5 sprigs fresh rosemary

FOR THE LAMB

8 small lamb noisettes

3 tablespoons mint jelly

FOR THE GRAVY

2 tablespoons plain flour

300 ml lamb stock or vegetable stock (see page 77)

Salt and black pepper to taste

Serves 4

Lamb noisettes are my first choice for this quick and simple supper dish, but if they prove hard to find, use lamb leg steaks instead which are readily available and just as delicious.

1   To prepare the potatoes, heat the oil over medium heat in a large saucepan that has a lid and add the new potatoes, sea salt and rosemary sprigs. Cover the pan and cook for 20 minutes, shaking the pan occasionally to prevent the potatoes from burning and sticking to the base of the pan.

2   Preheat the grill on a medium setting. To prepare the lamb, brush each of the noisettes on one side using half the mint jelly. Grill the lamb, jelly-side up, for 3 minutes. Then turn the lamb over, brush with the remaining jelly and grill the other side for a further 3 minutes until cooked through. Remove from the grill and keep warm.

3   To make the gravy, add the flour to the lamb juices in the grill pan and stir well. Gradually add the stock, then place the grill pan on the hob. Cook for 3–5 minutes to thicken the gravy, stirring constantly to prevent lumps from forming. Season with salt and black pepper to taste.

4   Serve the lamb noisettes hot with the crispy potatoes, gravy and mixed stir-fried vegetables.

BACON & MUSHROOM OMELETTE

Omelettes are one of the easiest dishes to cook. The fillings can be as elaborate or basic as you wish. Here I have chosen a simple filling of slightly browned smoked bacon with shiitake mushrooms (that are cooked in the bacon fat) and garlic. For extra flavour, I like to add a variety of fresh herbs to the egg mixture.

1 Place the bacon or pancetta in a frying pan and cook over low heat until the fat begins to run. Increase the heat and continue to cook for 3 minutes until the bacon begins to brown. Add the shiitake mushrooms and garlic and cook for a further 3 minutes, then set aside.

2 Lightly whisk the eggs in a bowl with 1 tablespoon of cold water. Add the chopped herbs and season with salt and black pepper.

3 Heat half the oil in a 20 cm omelette pan over medium heat and add half of the egg mixture. Tilt the pan or use a spatula to manipulate the egg mixture so it spreads to cover the base of the pan. Cook for 8–10 minutes.

4 Once the omelette is cooked, scatter half the bacon mixture over it. Fold the omelette in half while still in the pan and transfer to a warmed serving plate. Keep warm while making the second omelette using the remaining egg and bacon mixtures.

180 g smoked back bacon or pancetta, chopped

250 g shiitake mushrooms, trimmed and quartered

2 cloves garlic, peeled and chopped

4 eggs, medium-sized

2 tablespoons chopped fresh mixed herbs, such as parsley, tarragon or chives

Salt and black pepper to taste

1 tablespoon olive oil

Serves 2

PEPPER AND BEEF OMELETTE

Heat 1 tablespoon of sesame oil in a frying pan and add 1 halved and thinly sliced red pepper and 200 g of sliced lean fillet of beef. Cook over high heat for 5 minutes until the beef is sealed and the pepper is just beginning to soften. Whisk the eggs with 1 tablespoon of cold water, 1 tablespoon of chopped fresh oregano and 1 teaspoon of horseradish sauce. Cook as instructed above.

SMOKED SAUSAGE AND CARAMELIZED ONION OMELETTE

Heat 2 tablespoons of olive oil in a frying pan and add 2 peeled and sliced onions and 2 teaspoons of granulated sugar. Cook over medium heat for 10 minutes, stirring frequently. Add 2 thickly sliced chorizo sausages to the pan and continue to cook for a further 5 minutes, until the onions have caramelized to a rich golden colour and the sausages are heated through. Whisk the eggs with the water and cook as instructed above, adding the filling to the cooked omelettes before turning them on to warmed plates.

RATATOUILLE GRATIN

I large aubergine, weighing approximately 350 g, sliced

6 tablespoons olive oil

I large onion, peeled and sliced

3 cloves garlic, peeled and chopped

125 g mushrooms, cleaned and sliced

450 g courgettes, sliced

680 g tomatoes, quartered

2 tablespoons each chopped fresh thyme and marjoram

Salt and black pepper to taste

450 g potatoes, peeled and sliced

25 g freshly grated soya cheese

5–6 sprigs fresh rosemary

Serves 6

Traditional Provençal ratatouille is a combination of hearty vegetables that are cooked in olive oil, garlic and herbs. Here, I have topped this mixture with thinly sliced potatoes and soya cheese and baked the dish until the top is crispy and golden (see above).

1 Place the aubergine slices in a colander and sprinkle with 1–2 tablespoons of salt. Leave to stand for 10 minutes to draw out the bitter juices. Rinse the aubergine thoroughly with cold water and pat dry with kitchen paper.

2 Preheat the oven to 220°C, gas mark 7. Heat 4 tablespoons of the oil in a large frying pan and add the onion and garlic. Cook over high heat for 5 minutes until softened but not browned. Add the aubergine, mushrooms and courgettes and stir-fry for 5–8 minutes until they start to wilt.

3 Stir in the quartered tomatoes and herbs and cook for a further 5 minutes. Season the mixture with salt and black pepper and spoon it into a large ovenproof dish.

4 Arrange the potato slices over the vegetable mixture so that they overlap. Sprinkle with the grated soya cheese and drizzle with the remaining 2 tablespoons of oil. Scatter sprigs of rosemary over the top.

5 Bake in the preheated oven for 20 minutes until the top is crisp and golden and the ratatouille is bubbling. Serve immediately on its own as a main course or as a side dish with roast lamb.

TABBOULEH

Bulgar wheat, which is available from most good supermarkets and health food stores, is the main ingredient of this famous Middle Eastern salad. Chopped onions, tomatoes and a selection of herbs are also included, and I like to add meat or fish and chargrilled vegetables to make the dish less of a side dish and more of a meal-in-one.

1 Tip the bulgar wheat into a large heatproof bowl and pour in enough boiling water to cover. Leave to stand for 10 minutes until all the water has been absorbed by the wheat.

2 Place the diced ham, the chargrilled pepper, artichoke and aubergine and the tomatoes in a large bowl and mix together.

3 Run a fork through the bulgar wheat several times to separate the grains. Stir the ham and vegetable mixture into the bulgar wheat using a fork, then add the herbs, olive oil and lemon juice. Season with salt and black pepper and mix thoroughly. Serve immediately with a dressed green salad and crusty bread rolls.

250 g bulgar wheat

250 g cooked ham, diced

200 g chargrilled peppers, cut into strips

200 g chargrilled artichokes, chopped

200 g chargrilled aubergines, chopped

100 g tomatoes, cut into sixths

3 tablespoons chopped fresh Mediterranean herbs, such as basil, oregano and flat-leaf parsley

2 tablespoons olive oil

1 tablespoon lemon juice

Salt and black pepper to taste

Serves 6

SPINACH & POTATO CURRY

Fragrant spices such as turmeric, coriander, cumin and garam masala marry wonderfully with the flavours of the potatoes, baby spinach and fresh peas in this nutritious and hearty vegetarian meal.

1 Heat the oil in a large saucepan, then add the turmeric, garam masala and the coriander and cumin seeds. Cook the spices over medium heat for approximately 1 minute, stirring constantly until the spices are well blended with the oil.

2 Stir in the chopped onion and garlic and cook for a further 3–4 minutes. Then add the cubed potatoes and cook for another 3 minutes, stirring constantly until the potatoes are well coated in the oil and spices and just beginning to soften.

3 Pour the vegetable stock into the pan, then stir in the fresh peas. Bring the mixture to a boil, reduce the heat and simmer uncovered for 5 minutes.

4 When the stock has reduced and the potatoes are almost cooked, add the spinach and cook for roughly 3 minutes until it has wilted.

5 Stir in the fresh coriander and season with salt and black pepper. Serve the dish either on its own with warm naan bread or as an accompaniment to a meat curry.

2 tablespoons sunflower oil

1 teaspoon turmeric

½ teaspoon each of garam masala, ground coriander and cumin seeds

1 onion, peeled and finely chopped

2 cloves garlic, peeled and chopped

500 g potatoes, peeled and cubed

300 ml vegetable stock (see page 77)

250 g fresh peas

250 g baby spinach, trimmed and halved

2 tablespoons chopped fresh coriander

Salt and black pepper to taste

Serves 4

MUSHROOM & PARMA HAM PIZZA

It is no longer odd (in fact it is rather fashionable) to have pizzas without cheese on top – they can be just as filling and just as tasty. I like to top them with plenty of tomatoes, onions, mixed mushrooms and Parma ham. To complete, add your favourite herbs; rocket and flat-leaf parsley are particularly good (see right).

FOR THE BASE

175 g self-raising flour

1 teaspoon mustard powder

2 tablespoons chopped fresh herbs

Salt and black pepper to taste

2 eggs, medium-sized

3 tablespoons olive oil

FOR THE TOPPING

3 beef steak tomatoes, sliced

1 tablespoon olive oil

1 red onion, peeled and sliced

2 cloves garlic, peeled and sliced

250 g mixed mushrooms such as oyster, chestnut and shiitake, trimmed and sliced

80 g Parma ham, cut into 2.5 cm strips

30 g flat-leaf parsley or rocket

Black pepper to taste

Serves 4

1   Preheat the oven to 200°C, gas mark 6. To make the base, sift the flour into a bowl with the mustard powder and herbs. Season with salt and pepper and make a well in the centre of the mixture. Whisk together the eggs, olive oil and 2 teaspoons of cold water. Place the liquid in the well in the centre of the flour and mix the flour into it a little at a time, until a soft, not sticky, dough is formed. Roll out the dough on a lightly floured surface to a 23 x 18 cm rectangle. Transfer the pizza base to a baking sheet.

2   Arrange the sliced beef steak tomatoes on top of the pizza base. Heat the oil in a large frying pan and add the onions and garlic. Cook over medium heat for 5 minutes until the onions are softened but not coloured. Stir in the mushrooms and cook for a further 2–3 minutes. Then spoon the mushroom mixture over the tomatoes on the pizza base and arrange the strips of Parma ham on top.

3   Bake the pizza in the preheated oven for 20 minutes, until the base is cooked and golden around the edges and the topping is piping hot.

4   Remove the pizza from the oven and immediately top with flat-leaf parsley or rocket. Season with black pepper. Serve drizzled with a little more olive oil, if desired, and a fresh green salad.

CHUNKY SPANISH OMELETTE

Traditionally a Spanish dish, this chunky omelette is also known as a Tortilla and is usually served either warm or cold as a light lunch or as part of 'tapas' (a selection of savoury nibbles) with a glass of chilled medium-dry sherry.

4 tablespoons olive oil

350 g cooked potatoes, diced

1 leek, finely sliced

6 eggs, medium-sized

Salt and black pepper to taste

125 g fresh peas

125 g broccoli florets

Serves 4

1   Heat the oil in a 23 cm non-stick frying pan over medium heat, add the potatoes and leek and cook for 5 minutes until the leek is translucent.

2   Beat the eggs with the seasoning, then stir in the fried vegetables, peas and broccoli until they are all coated in the egg. Pour the mixture into the pan and cook over medium heat for 12–15 minutes until the top of the omelette begins to set and the bottom is cooked. Place the pan under a medium-hot grill and cook the top side of the omelette until set. Serve cut into wedges.

3 Main Meals

FISH

_____

POULTRY

_____

MEAT

_____

VEGETABLES

HADDOCK WITH BEETROOT

FOR THE BEETROOT

500 g raw beetroot

Grated rind and juice of 1 orange

FOR THE FISH

4 haddock fillets (or turbot steaks), each weighing 175 g

Salt and black pepper to taste

2 tablespoons olive oil

2 tablespoons chopped fresh parsley

Serves 4

Haddock fillets are pan-fried in olive oil and parsley and served on a bed of thinly sliced beetroot which is flavoured with a hint of orange. This dish shows that beetroot – often an underrated vegetable – can be an exciting and colourful addition to a meal. To vary the fish, use turbot steaks in place of haddock fillets.

1 To prepare the beetroot, peel and cut it into matchsticks. Bring a saucepan of water to a boil and add 1 tablespoon of orange juice. Add the beetroot and cook for 5 minutes until it begins to soften. Drain and set aside.

2 Place the remaining orange juice and the rind in a frying pan and cook over medium heat until bubbling. Then, add the beetroot and cook for a further 5 minutes, stirring frequently. Remove from the heat and set aside.

3 Season the fillets with salt and black pepper. Heat the oil in a frying pan and add the fish. Cook over medium heat for 5 minutes, turning once, until the fish is golden and the flesh flakes easily. Divide the beetroot between 4 serving plates, place a haddock fillet on top and garnish with parsley.

SEARED TUNA WITH MIXED BEAN SALAD

FOR THE FISH

4 tuna steaks, each weighing 200 g

Grated rind of 1 lemon

2 tablespoons chopped fresh parsley, chervil or dill

Salt and black pepper to taste

2 tablespoons olive oil

FOR THE SALAD

800 g cooked mixed beans and pulses

1 red onion, peeled and chopped

75 ml Vinaigrette Dressing (see below, right)

Salt and black pepper to taste

Serves 4

Fresh tuna has a rich flavour and meaty texture. Here, it is cooked with simplicity in plenty of sizzling olive oil with a dash of lemon and a few chopped fresh herbs.

1 To prepare the tuna, rinse the steaks, pat dry and set aside. Mix together the lemon rind and your chosen herb in a bowl and season with salt and black pepper. Stir in the oil and mix until the ingredients are thoroughly blended. Spread half the lemon mixture on one side of the tuna steaks.

2 Arrange the steaks, lemon-side down, on a griddle pan. Cook over high heat for 3 minutes, until golden. Spread the uncooked side of the tuna with the remaining lemon mixture, turn over and cook for a further 3 minutes.

3 Combine the mixed beans and pulses, chopped onion and Vinaigrette Dressing in a bowl. Season to taste. Divide the bean salad between 4 plates, place the tuna steaks on top and serve immediately.

VINAIGRETTE DRESSING
Place 4 tablespoons olive oil, 2 tablespoons lemon juice, 3 tablespoons chopped fresh parsley and half a teaspoon of caster sugar in a bowl and whisk until all the ingredients are well blended. Season to taste with salt and black pepper.

WARM SCALLOP & AVOCADO SALAD

Scallops are easy to prepare and have a meaty texture and sweet, succulent flavour that is irresistible. Here, they are combined with crunchy walnuts, creamy avocados, fine beans and a tart lemon and mustard dressing (see below) in a salad that is perfect for relaxed summer meals with friends. This is the ideal dish for giving your guests an extra-special treat.

1 Heat the oils in a large frying pan and add the scallops and beans. Stir-fry over high heat for 5 minutes until the scallops brown on the outside but remain soft and juicy in the middle. Meanwhile, peel, stone and coarsely chop the avocados.

2 Add the chopped avocados and the walnut pieces to the pan. Continue to cook for 2 minutes, stirring frequently. Remove the pan from the heat and stir in the lemon juice and wholegrain mustard. Season to taste with salt and black pepper.

3 Divide the mixed salad leaves between 4 plates and arrange the scallop mixture on top. Serve immediately.

4 tablespoons walnut oil

4 tablespoons sunflower oil

500 g cleaned scallops

100 g French beans, trimmed and cut into 2.5 cm pieces

2 avocados

75 g walnut pieces

Juice of 1 small lemon

1 teaspoon wholegrain honey mustard

Salt and black pepper to taste

100 g mixed salad leaves, washed

Serves 4

POACHED SALMON WITH FRESH HERB DRESSING

6 salmon cutlets

1 bottle white wine

1 onion, peeled and quartered

2 sticks celery, roughly chopped

4 sprigs fresh parsley

6 peppercorns

½ lemon, sliced

22 g aspic

5 cm piece cucumber, thinly sliced

6 sprigs fresh dill to serve

Serves 6

This is a quick and easy version of the classic whole poached salmon. By using salmon cutlets, the dish is ready in half the time but still looks impressive (see above) and, of course, tastes just as fabulous.

1 Place the salmon cutlets in a frying pan that has a lid and add the wine, onion, celery, parsley, peppercorns and lemon. Bring to a boil, reduce the heat and simmer covered for 10 minutes. Remove the pan from the heat and leave to cool – the salmon continues to cook gently as the liquid cools.

2 Dissolve the aspic according to the packet instructions and leave to cool and set. Remove the skin from the salmon and gently pull out the centre bone using your fingers. Brush a layer of thickened aspic over the salmon and arrange the cucumber and dill decoratively on top. Brush again with aspic and chill in the refrigerator for 30 minutes before serving.

3 Serve the salmon with the herb dressing (see below), fresh peas, beans and Seared New Potatoes (see page 65).

HERB DRESSING
Beat together 150 ml mayonnaise with 3 tablespoons chopped fresh dill in a mixing bowl. Season to taste with salt and freshly ground black pepper. Cover and chill in the refrigerator for up to 4 hours. Use as required.

ROAST MONKFISH WITH GREEN LENTILS

Lentils are an ancient source of nourishment that has been cultivated, it is believed, for 8,000 years, since neolithic times. Here, this healthy and non-fattening pulse makes the perfect partner for the meaty flesh and mild, slightly sweet flavour of monkfish.

1 Preheat the oven to 190°C, gas mark 5. Heat the oil in a saucepan and add the onions. Cook over medium heat for 5 minutes until they begin to soften. Add the green lentils and stir well.

2 Cut 4 slices from one of the lemons and set aside. Squeeze the juice from the remaining lemons. Add the juice to the pan with the lentils, stir in the chopped parsley and season with salt and black pepper. Continue to cook for 5 minutes until all the ingredients are heated through.

3 Meanwhile, cut the reserved lemon slices in half and tie 2 half-slices and a sprig of rosemary on to each piece of fish with string. Wrap the pieces of monkfish in foil and bake in the preheated oven for 8–10 minutes until the fish is opaque and the flesh begins to flake.

4 Remove the fish from the oven, carefully remove the string, lemon and rosemary and serve on a bed of warm green lentils.

FOR THE LENTILS

1 tablespoon sunflower oil

2 red onions, peeled and cut into eighths

2 cans green lentils, each weighing 420 g, rinsed and drained

2 lemons

3 tablespoons chopped fresh parsley

Salt and black pepper to taste

FOR THE FISH

4 boned monkfish tails, each weighing 175 g

4 sprigs fresh rosemary

Serves 4

RED MULLET WITH GOOSEBERRIES

The tartness of gooseberries brings a lively tang to this recipe which goes well with the fish. If possible, try to buy the mullet with the liver still intact as this has a wonderful flavour.

1 Clean the mullet thoroughly (leaving the liver intact, if possible). Trim the fins and tail and make two or three slashes in the sides of each fish with a sharp knife. Spoon a little ginger into each cavity and season the fish with salt and black pepper.

2 Heat the olive oil in a large frying pan and add the red mullet. Cook over high heat for 2 minutes on each side. Add the gooseberries and cook for 5–10 minutes until they begin to pop.

3 Add the sugar and wine to the pan and cook for a further 5 minutes, stirring frequently until the fish is cooked through and the sauce has thickened slightly. Season with salt and black pepper to taste and serve with boiled new potatoes and steamed green vegetables.

4 red mullet, each weighing 450 g

3 cm piece root ginger, peeled and chopped

Salt and black pepper to taste

1 tablespoon olive oil

375 g gooseberries, topped and tailed

40 g caster sugar

150 ml white wine

Serves 4

Paella

Chicken, vegetables, herbs and a variety of seafood are cooked with saffron rice in this popular Spanish dish (see inset, right). Here, the chicken is boiled and the water is used for the stock – even though this takes time, it is an important step which gives the dish more flavour. Substitute the chicken with a 500 g joint of bacon for an alternative.

1 Place the chicken breasts in a shallow pan with the onion, bay leaves, peppercorns, saffron and parsley. Cover with cold water and bring slowly to a boil. Reduce the heat and simmer for 30 minutes. Leave to cool for 10 minutes. Strain and discard all but the liquid and the chicken.

2 When cool enough to handle, dice the chicken and set aside. Add sufficient cold water to the reserved liquid (stock) to make the quantity up to 900 ml.

3 To prepare the rice, heat the oil in a medium-sized paella pan or large shallow frying pan and add the onion and garlic. Fry over medium heat until softened, not browned. Add the rice and stir until the grains are well coated in the oil.

4 Pour in 1 ladleful of chicken stock and wait for the liquid to be fully absorbed before adding the next ladleful. Continue in this way, stirring occasionally, until the rice has absorbed half the original quantity of stock.

5 Finally, add the remaining chicken stock with the mussels, diced chicken, cooked prawns, parsley and peas. Season with salt and black pepper and mix well so all the ingredients are combined. Simmer for 15–20 minutes, stirring occasionally, until all the chicken stock has been absorbed by the rice and the vegetables are thoroughly cooked and the mussel shells have opened. Serve immediately, directly from the pan.

FOR THE CHICKEN

4 chicken breasts, skinned and boned

1 onion, peeled and quartered

2 bay leaves

6 peppercorns

1 teaspoon saffron strands

Bunch of fresh parsley

FOR THE RICE

2 tablespoons olive oil

1 onion, peeled and chopped

3 cloves garlic, peeled and crushed

375 g Arborio risotto rice

450 g fresh mussels, cleaned

125 g jumbo prawns, cooked

2 tablespoons chopped fresh parsley

250 g fresh peas

Salt and black pepper to taste

Serves 6

Fennel-stuffed Sea Bass

Sea bass is infused with the flavours of fennel, spring onions and thyme when the whole ensemble is baked together in a paper pocket.

1 Preheat the oven to 200°C, gas mark 6. Cut 6 sheets of greaseproof paper into large heart-shapes at least double the size of each fish. Cut the fish into 12 fillets and season with salt and freshly ground black pepper.

2 Lay 1 fillet, skin-side down on each sheet of greaseproof paper. Scatter each fillet with fennel and spring onions and drizzle with olive oil. Place a sprig of thyme on top of the fillet and cover with another fillet, skin-side up. Bring the sides of the greaseproof paper together to enclose the fish and fold or twist the edges over to seal. Bake in the preheated oven for 15 minutes until the flesh is opaque and flakes easily.

6 sea bass, each weighing 450 g

Salt and black pepper to taste

2 small bulbs fennel, trimmed and sliced

4 spring onions, trimmed and sliced

2 tablespoons olive oil

6 sprigs fresh thyme

Serves 6

TURKEY WITH PRESERVED LEMONS & COUSCOUS

1 kg turkey breast, skinned and boned

Salt and black pepper to taste

Grated rind and juice of 1 lemon

2 cloves garlic, peeled and chopped

3 tablespoons olive oil

6 shallots, peeled and quartered

175 g chestnut mushrooms, halved

2 courgettes, medium-sized, sliced

150 ml each of white wine and chicken stock (see page 77)

6 sun-dried tomatoes, sliced

8 preserved lemon wedges (see opposite)

This exotic dish of turkey cooked with lemon, garlic, white wine and vegetables is served on a bed of parsley-flavoured couscous (see below).

1   Place the turkey in a shallow dish. Stir in the salt and black pepper, lemon rind and juice and garlic. Cover and leave to marinate for 30 minutes.

2   Heat the oil in a large flameproof casserole and add the shallots. Cook over medium heat until the shallots begin to brown, then add the mushrooms and courgettes and continue to cook for a further 5 minutes. Remove the vegetables using a slotted spoon and set aside.

3   Add the turkey to the casserole and cook for roughly 15 minutes until brown on all sides. Return the shallots, mushrooms and courgettes to the casserole, pour in the wine and stock and bring to a boil.

4   Once the liquid is boiling, stir in the tomatoes, then reduce the heat and cook for 10 minutes. Add the lemon and cook for a further 15 minutes, until the turkey is cooked through. Season with salt and black pepper.

5   To prepare the couscous, bring the stock to a boil in a saucepan that has a lid. Add the couscous, stir, then remove from the heat. Cover and leave to stand for 15 minutes until the couscous has absorbed the stock. Separate the grains with a fork, stir in the parsley and season with salt and black pepper. Divide the couscous between 4 plates and top with some turkey.

FOR THE COUSCOUS

350 ml chicken stock (see page 77)

350 g couscous

3 tablespoons chopped fresh parsley

Salt and black pepper to taste

Serves 4

PRESERVING LEMONS

Wash 500 g unwaxed lemons. Mark them into quarters and using a knife, cut almost to the centre of each lemon, leaving them intact. Ease the cuts apart and spread 1 teaspoon salt inside each cut. Pack the lemons into a 500 g preserving jar and place a disc of baking parchment (cut to size) on top. Weight down the lemons using jars and leave for 4 days in a warm room. Remove the weights and parchment, pour over enough lemon juice to cover the lemons, then pour over 2 tablespoons olive oil to form a thin layer. Seal and leave for 1 month.

COQ AU VIN

Chicken, bacon, onions and red wine make up this popular French dish which is traditionally thickened with softened butter and flour (beurre manié), so beware of this dish when eating out. However, rather than abstaining altogether, try this irresistible lactose-free version.

1   Immerse the onions in boiling water for 1 minute, then plunge them into cold water – the skins should now peel off easily and without any tears.

2   To prepare the chicken, heat the oil in a large flameproof casserole. Add the onions and cook over medium heat for 5 minutes until golden. Stir in the bacon, garlic and mushrooms and cook for a further 10 minutes, stirring frequently. Remove the vegetables and bacon from the casserole using a slotted spoon and set aside.

3   Place the chicken pieces in batches in the casserole. Cook them over medium heat on all sides for 15 minutes until the skin turns golden.

4   Stir the cornflour into the casserole. Cook over low heat until the chicken begins to brown. Return the vegetables and bacon to the casserole, then pour in the wine and mix well to ensure the cornflour is blended with the wine thoroughly.

5   To prepare the bouquet garni, place the herbs and peppercorns in a square of muslin. Draw the edges of the fabric up around the herbs to form a sack and tie with string, leaving a length of string to tie around the handle of the casserole for easy removal. Add the bouquet garni to the casserole and bring the liquid to a boil, then simmer for 30–40 minutes. Season with salt and black pepper and garnish with chopped parsley to serve. This dish is delicious served with potatoes mashed with olive oil.

FOR THE CHICKEN

12 baby onions

3 tablespoons sunflower oil

250 g rindless streaky bacon, chopped

3 cloves garlic, peeled and crushed

250 g button mushrooms, cleaned and halved

6 chicken thighs, boned

3 chicken breasts, boned and halved

1 tablespoon cornflour

1 bottle red wine

Salt and black pepper to taste

3 tablespoons chopped fresh parsley

FOR THE BOUQUET GARNI

1 sprig each fresh parsley, thyme and sage

1 bay leaf

4 peppercorns

Serves 6

THAI GREEN CURRY

Lean white meat is cooked in coconut milk and green curry paste, which gives it a distinctive flavour that is both sweet and spicy at the same time. Chicken or turkey breasts are ideal for this dish, which should be served hot with plenty of boiled rice and garnished with fresh herbs and red chilli.

4 green chillies, halved and deseeded

1 stalk lemon grass, sliced

3 shallots, peeled and halved

3 cloves garlic, peeled and halved

2 cm piece galangal (Thai ginger), peeled and chopped

Grated rind of ½ lime

1 teaspoon each coriander and cumin seeds

1 teaspoon shrimp paste

400 ml canned coconut milk

6 chicken breasts or 3 turkey breasts, weighing 1 kg, skinned and boned

2 tablespoons fish sauce

1 tablespoon soft light brown sugar

1 red chilli, deseeded and thinly sliced, grated rind of 1 lime and chopped fresh sweet basil or coriander to garnish

Serves 6

1 To make the curry paste, place the green chillies, lemon grass, shallots, garlic, galangal, lime rind, coriander and cumin seeds and shrimp paste in a food processor and blend to form a thick green paste. With the motor still running, gradually add half of the coconut milk and then process until all the ingredients are well combined. (Alternatively, pound the ingredients in a mortar with a pestle until a thick paste is formed, then add the milk.)

2 Place the remaining coconut milk in a large frying pan and bring to a boil, then simmer for 5 minutes until reduced to half the original quantity. Stir in the prepared green curry paste and simmer for a further 5 minutes.

3 Slice the chicken breasts thinly and add to the frying pan containing the reduced coconut milk. Stir in the fish sauce and brown sugar and simmer for 10 minutes. The mixture will take on a slightly curdled look during cooking – this is normal. Once the chicken is tender and cooked through, serve it immediately. Divide the chicken into 6 portions and place them on individual servings of plain boiled rice. Garnish each portion with strips of red chilli, a sprinkling of lime rind and chopped basil or coriander.

MONKFISH CURRY

Monkfish, which has a meaty texture and mild flavour, makes an excellent alternative to chicken or turkey breasts in Thai Green Curry, above. Cut 1 kg of monkfish into cubes and cook as for the chicken.

TURKEY TIKKA

This simple supper dish of marinated and grilled turkey fillets can be prepared in advance and takes only minutes to cook.

2 turkey breast fillets, halved

4 tablespoons plain soya yogurt

2 tablespoons concentrated tikka paste

1 lime, cut into wedges and a handful of fresh coriander leaves to garnish

Serves 2

1 Place the halved turkey fillets between 2 sheets of greaseproof paper and carefully flatten them into escalopes using a rolling pin.

2 Mix together the yogurt and tikka paste and spread on to both sides of the escalopes. (Cover and chill for up to 8 hours at this point, if desired.)

3 Preheat the grill to the highest setting and grill the turkey for 5–7 minutes on each side until crispy on the outside and cooked through. Garnish with lime wedges and coriander leaves and serve on a bed of steamed rice.

PHEASANT PIE

A contemporary version of a classic English dish, this recipe combines pheasant and hearty vegetables under a 'pastry' crust, proving once and for all that cooking without dairy products need not be a limitation.

2 pheasants
2 tablespoons olive oil
I leek, trimmed and sliced
250 g parsnips, peeled and sliced
250 g carrots, peeled and sliced
I bulb fennel, trimmed and sliced
2 tablespoons flour
Grated rind and juice of 2 oranges
300 ml chicken stock (see page 77)
3 tablespoons chopped fresh parsley
Salt and black pepper to taste
500 g shortcrust pastry (see below)
I egg yolk to glaze
Serves 4

1. Bone the pheasants and cut the meat into chunks. Heat the oil in a large flameproof casserole and add the leek, parsnips, carrots and fennel. Cook over medium heat for 10 minutes, stirring frequently. Then remove the vegetables from the casserole using a slotted spoon and set aside.

2. Add the pheasant meat to the casserole and stir-fry over high heat for 10 minutes, until browned. Sprinkle the flour over the meat and add the grated rind and juice of the oranges and the stock. Mix well to combine all the ingredients. Return the vegetables to the casserole with the parsley and season with salt and black pepper. Slowly bring to a boil, reduce the heat and simmer for 20 minutes.

3. Meanwhile, preheat the oven to 200°C, gas mark 6 and prepare the pastry (see below). Then place 4 individual 450 ml pie dishes on a baking tray and divide the cooked pheasant mixture between the dishes.

4. Divide the pastry into 4 and roll out each piece on a lightly floured work surface until large enough to cover each pie. Use the pastry trimmings to make a rim around each dish, then dampen the pastry rim with cold water and cover with a pastry lid. Pinch the edges together to seal, then brush the tops of the pies with beaten egg yolk to glaze. Make a small hole in the pastry to allow steam to escape. Bake in the preheated oven for 20 minutes until the pastry is golden brown. Serve immediately with Caramelized Apple Rings (see below) and shredded and steamed Savoy cabbage.

CARAMELIZED APPLE RINGS

Core 4 eating apples and slice into thin rings. Heat 4 tablespoons of olive oil in a frying pan and stir in 2 tablespoons of icing sugar. Add the apple rings and cook over high heat for 4–5 minutes until the apples brown and soften. Warm 3 tablespoons of Calvados in a separate saucepan and ignite it with a lit taper. Pour the flaming alcohol over the apples and stir until the flames die down.

SHORTCRUST PASTRY

Sieve 350 g of plain flour into a bowl. Add a pinch of salt and 175 g dairy-free margarine. Rub in the margarine with your fingertips until it resembles fine breadcrumbs. Add 1 egg yolk and continue to mix. Then stir in sufficient iced water until a soft but not sticky dough is formed. (Alternatively, place all the ingredients into a food processor and blend.) Turn out the pastry on to a floured work surface and knead. Shape the dough into a ball, wrap it in clingfilm and chill in the refrigerator for 30 minutes before use. (Makes 500 g.)

POUSSIN WITH STICKY GLAZE

Chickens that are sold for the table between the ages of four and six weeks old were called 'spring chickens', but nowadays, butchers and supermarkets use the French expression 'poussin'. They are lean and tasty and – with this sauce based on orange liqueur – utterly delicious.

1   Preheat the oven to 220°C, gas mark 7. Pack the poussin into a roasting tin. Mix together the oil, honey, juniper berries and the rind and juice of the clementine in a bowl. Season with salt and black pepper. Stir the mixture until well combined, then spoon it over the poussin. Roast the poussin in the preheated oven for 40 minutes, basting occasionally.

2   Place the cooked poussin on to a serving platter and cover with foil to keep warm. To prepare the sauce, place the chopped onion into the roasting tin the poussin was cooked in and cook on the hob over high heat until they begin to brown. Add the Cointreau to the tin and boil until the mixture reduces by half.

3   Remove the inner pith from the clementine rind, then cut it into thin strips. Heat the oil in a frying pan and cook the strips until crispy. When ready to serve, spoon this glaze over the poussin. Serve with the sauce, Fennel and Mangetout Stir-fry (see page 72) and Seared New Potatoes (see page 65).

FOR THE POUSSIN

4 poussin

2 tablespoons olive oil

2 tablespoons clear honey

2 teaspoons juniper berries, crushed

Rind and juice of 1 clementine

Salt and black pepper to taste

FOR THE SAUCE

1 onion, peeled and finely chopped

5 teaspoons Cointreau

Rind of 1 clementine

1 tablespoon olive oil

Serves 4

DUCK WITH CRANBERRIES

Cranberries (see inset, left) are best eaten between October and December and their tartness goes very well with succulent, sweet marmalade-coated duck breasts (see left).

1   Pierce the duck skin in several places gently with a fork. Place the duck breasts, skin-side down, in a large frying pan and cook over low heat until the fat trapped between the skin and the flesh begins to run. Increase the heat to a medium setting and cook for 5 minutes on each side until the skin is crisp and golden. Drain all but roughly 2 tablespoons of the fat and add the shallot to the pan. Cook for 3 minutes until transparent.

2   Brush the duck breasts with the marmalade, then cook them over very high heat until the marmalade coating caramelizes (this process seals in the meat's juices to prevent it drying out during cooking).

3   Mix 1 tablespoon of the orange juice with the arrowroot until smooth. Add it to the pan with the cranberries and the grated rind and remaining juice of the orange. Mix well, reduce the heat and simmer for 10 minutes until the cranberries pop and the juice reduces by half and thickens. Stir in the thyme and season with salt and black pepper. Serve with boiled pink fir potatoes and stir-fried green cabbage with caraway seeds, if desired.

4 duck fillets

1 shallot, peeled and finely chopped

4 tablespoons thick-cut marmalade

Grated rind and juice of 2 oranges

1 teaspoon arrowroot

225 g fresh or frozen cranberries

2 tablespoons chopped fresh thyme

Salt and black pepper to taste

Serves 4

VENISON & VEGETABLE POT PIES

FOR THE FILLING

2 tablespoons sunflower oil

1 onion, peeled and sliced

2 sticks celery, rinsed and chopped

225 g parsnips, peeled and chopped

100 g carrots, scrubbed and sliced

1 tablespoon plain flour

½ teaspoon dried rosemary

675 g venison, diced

300 ml game stock

2 tablespoons chopped fresh parsley

FOR THE PASTRY TOPPING

120 g filo pastry, 8 sheets measuring approximately 40 x 30 cm

1 egg, beaten, to glaze

Serves 4

These individual venison and winter vegetable casseroles are topped with paper-thin filo pastry and are impressive enough to serve at a dinner party. They can be made well in advance, assembled and frozen for up to one month. When it comes to entertaining, all you need to do is thaw the pies in the refrigerator for twelve hours, then place them in a preheated oven as your guests arrive.

1 Preheat the oven to 200°C, gas mark 6. To prepare the filling, heat the oil in a large saucepan and add the onion and the celery. Cook over medium heat for 3–4 minutes until softened but not browned. Stir in the parsnips and carrots and cook for a further 5 minutes. Remove the vegetables from the pan using a slotted spoon and set aside.

2 Place the flour and rosemary in a large plastic food bag. Add the diced venison to the bag, then seal and shake it vigorously until the meat is evenly coated with the seasoned flour. Place the venison in the saucepan that was used to cook the vegetables and cook in the hot oil over high heat until brown on all sides.

3 Return the vegetables to the pan with the game stock and the chopped parsley. Stir well, reduce the heat and simmer covered for 40 minutes, stirring frequently. Remove the pan from the heat and divide the venison mixture between 4 ovenproof 300 ml ramekins.

4 To prepare the pastry, cut the filo sheets into squares that are large enough to easily fit over the top of each pie. Brush the rim of each ramekin with beaten egg and layer 4 filo pastry sheets on top of each pie, pressing them down on to the rims of the ramekins to seal the ingredients. Place the ramekins on a baking tray and bake in the preheated oven for 10 minutes until the pastry is golden. Serve immediately with green vegetables.

LAMB OR PORK POT PIES

Substitute the venison with 675 g of either diced lamb or pork and follow the recipe above, using lamb stock (see page 77) or pork stock as appropriate.

VEGETABLE POT PIES

Substitute the venison with a 675 g mixture of peeled and diced sweet potato and beetroot. Use 300 ml vegetable stock (see page 77) in place of game stock.

CHILLI BEEF SALAD

The strong flavours of spicy red chillies, sweet cherry tomatoes, woody shiitake mushrooms and toasted sesame seeds combine to create a wonderfully hot and tasty beef salad (see above).

1 Grill the beef under a hot grill for 1–4 minutes, depending on how well you like your meat cooked. Leave to cool, then slice as thinly as possible.

2 Deseed and slice the chillies, then slice the mushrooms. Heat the oil in a frying pan, add the chillies and mushrooms and stir-fry over high heat for 5 minutes, stirring occasionally.

3 Place the sesame seeds in a heavy-based frying pan and cook over low heat for 1–2 minutes, stirring occasionally until the seeds are toasted. Arrange the lettuce and chicory leaves, tomatoes and cucumber on 4 serving plates. Place the beef slices and mushroom mixture over the salad and scatter the sesame seeds over each portion. Serve with crusty bread rolls.

500 g beef steak

1 red and 1 yellow chilli

125 g shiitake mushrooms

2 tablespoons olive oil

2 tablespoons sesame seeds

1 green lettuce, washed and sliced

1 head chicory

125 g cherry tomatoes, halved

3 cm piece of cucumber, thinly sliced

Serves 4

LAMB TIKKA

Tikka is the Indian equivalent of the Turkish kebab, in that pieces of meat (usually chicken or lamb) are marinated in a spicy tikka paste, threaded on to skewers and then grilled. As the paste cooks, it creates a highly tasty coating for the nuggets of tender meat.

1   Cut the lamb into 5 cm cubes and place in a shallow dish. Blend the oil, tikka paste, garlic and coconut milk in a bowl. Pour the mixture over the lamb and toss to coat the meat evenly. Cover and leave to marinate at room temperature for 30 minutes or chill in the refrigerator for up to 12 hours.

2   Soak 8 wooden skewers in water to prevent them scorching. Remove the lamb from the marinade and divide into 8 piles. Thread each pile on to a skewer. Cook the kebabs under a medium hot grill for 5–10 minutes on each side until the meat is brown on the outside and cooked through.

3   Cook the rice according to the packet instructions, adding the turmeric to the cooking water. Garnish the kebabs with coriander and serve with the turmeric rice, mini naans and fruit chutney.

900 g lean lamb

2 tablespoons olive oil

2 tablespoons concentrated tikka paste

2 cloves garlic, peeled and coarsely chopped

150 ml coconut milk

300 g basmati rice

½ teaspoon powdered turmeric

Chopped fresh coriander to garnish

4 mini naan breads and fruit chutney to serve

Serves 4

ROAST LAMB WITH SHIITAKE STUFFING

The Japanese have made use of the meaty flesh and full-bodied, woody flavour of shiitake mushrooms for over 2,000 years. Here, they give the traditional English dish of roasted rack of lamb (see left) additional flavour with an exotic hint of the East.

1   Preheat the oven to 220°C, gas mark 7. To prepare the stuffing, heat the oil in a frying pan and add the spring onions and garlic. Cook over medium heat for 5 minutes until softened, not browned. Add the mushrooms and ginger and cook for a further 5 minutes, stirring frequently. Remove the pan from the heat and leave the mixture to cool. Once cool, stir well, then beat in the egg yolk and rosemary and season with salt and black pepper.

2   To prepare the lamb, season it with salt and black pepper and spread with the cranberry sauce. Spoon the stuffing into the centre of a roasting tin and set the two racks of lamb on top.

3   Place the lamb in the preheated oven and roast for either 30 minutes for rare lamb, or for 45 minutes if you like your lamb fairly well done. When ready to serve, remove the lamb from the oven and cut between the ribs to separate the meat into cutlets. Divide the stuffing into 4 portions, place on serving plates and arrange the lamb cutlets attractively around the stuffing. Serve with a side dish of mixed baby vegetables and chargrilled polenta.

1 tablespoon olive oil

4 spring onions, trimmed, quartered and cut into 2.5 cm lengths

2 cloves garlic, peeled and crushed

100 g shiitake mushrooms

2.5 cm root ginger, peeled and chopped

1 egg yolk

1 tablespoon chopped fresh rosemary

Salt and black pepper to taste

2 racks of lamb, trimmed

1 tablespoon cranberry sauce

Serves 4

LAMB & APRICOT COBBLER

Dried apricots add sweetness to this exotic and warming lamb, mushroom and cranberry casserole. It is topped with a tasty seasoned scone crust which finishes the dish off neatly and makes it a more substantial meal.

FOR THE CASSEROLE

2 tablespoons olive oil

1 onion, peeled and coarsely chopped

250 g chestnut mushrooms, sliced

1 tablespoon plain flour

1 teaspoon mixed spice

700 g lean lamb, cubed

300 ml lamb stock (see page 77)

175 g dried apricots

175 g fresh or frozen cranberries

Salt and black pepper to taste

FOR THE SCONE TOPPING

175 g self-raising flour

1 teaspoon baking powder

40 g non-dairy margarine

1 egg, medium-sized

2 tablespoons chopped fresh parsley

Serves 4

1 To prepare the casserole, heat the oil in a large flameproof casserole and add the onion and mushrooms. Cook over low heat until softened.

2 Place the flour and mixed spice into a large food bag and add the cubed lamb. Seal the bag and shake it vigorously to coat the meat evenly in the seasoned flour mixture.

3 Add the seasoned lamb to the pan with onions and mushrooms and stir. Increase the heat to a high setting and cook for 5–10 minutes until the lamb is evenly browned.

4 Add the stock to the pan and slowly bring to a boil. Reduce the heat and simmer for 15 minutes, stirring occasionally. Finally, stir in the apricots and cranberries and simmer for a further 5 minutes. Remove from the heat and set aside.

5 Preheat the oven to 200°C, gas mark 6. To prepare the scone topping, sift the flour and baking powder into a mixing bowl. Rub in the fat with your fingertips until the mixture resembles fine breadcrumbs. Beat together the egg, 4 tablespoons cold water and the parsley in a separate bowl, then add to the flour mixture. Mix until a soft, not sticky, dough is formed. Roll out the dough on a lightly floured work surface until roughly 2 cm-thick and cut out several 5 cm circles.

6 Arrange the scone shapes around the edge of the hot lamb casserole. Then bake in the preheated oven for 25 minutes until the scones are puffed and golden brown. Serve the Lamb & Apricot Cobbler with green beans.

WHOLEMEAL SCONE TOPPING

Substitute the self-raising flour with 175 g self-raising wholemeal flour. Sift it with the baking powder and rub in the fat with your fingertips as in step 5, above. Beat the egg with 5 tablespoons of cold water and 2 tablespoons of toasted sunflower seeds (in place of the parsley). The wholemeal topping makes this dish more substantial, for those extra chilly winter evenings!

FRUITY RABBIT CASSEROLE
Substitute the pork in Fruity Pork Casserole (see below) with 2 jointed rabbits. Cut the meat into cubes and place in a food bag with the flour and 1 teaspoon mustard powder (in place of mixed spice). Substitute the apricots with an equal quantity of prunes and cook as below. Serve with couscous. Rabbit has a mild flavour which is delicious with the spiced fruits.

FRUITY PORK CASSEROLE

During the cold winter months, one of the easiest ways of entertaining is with a hearty pork casserole that can bubble away happily on the stove until you are ready to eat. In this recipe, cubes of lean pork are cooked slowly with dried apricots, spices and plenty of red wine until the meat is very tender and succulent (see above).

1 Place the flour and mixed spice into a large food bag and add the cubed pork. Seal the bag and shake it vigorously to coat the meat evenly in the seasoned flour mixture. Heat half the oil in a large flameproof casserole over medium heat. Cook the meat in batches for roughly 10 minutes, until the meat is evenly browned. Remove the last batch from the casserole using a slotted spoon and set aside with the rest of the browned meat.

2 Heat the remaining oil in the casserole. Add the onion and celery and cook over high heat for 5 minutes, until the onions are softened, but not browned. Add the mushrooms and continue to cook for a further 3–4 minutes, stirring continuously.

3 Return the browned pork to the casserole with the apricots, raisins, apples and grated rind and juice of the orange and mix thoroughly. Add the red wine and parsley and season with salt and black pepper.

4 Bring the liquid in the casserole to a boil, then simmer uncovered for 2–2½ hours, stirring occasionally, until the meat is tender and the liquid is thickened. Serve Fruity Pork Casserole with couscous (see page 49).

25 g plain flour

1 teaspoon mixed spice

900 g lean pork, cubed

3 tablespoons sunflower oil

1 large onion, peeled and finely chopped

2 sticks celery

100 g chestnut mushrooms, sliced

100 g ready-to-eat apricots, halved

50 g raisins

2 apples, peeled, cored and chopped

Grated rind and juice of 1 orange

1 bottle red wine

3 tablespoons chopped fresh flat-leaf parsley

Salt and black pepper to taste

Serves 6

VEGETABLE STIR-FRY

This is a delicious and healthy vegetarian main course, which is packed with fresh, crunchy vegetables and cooked very rapidly in hot oil. This Oriental style of cooking food has recently become extremely popular and is one of the fastest and most nutritious methods of cooking. You do not necessarily need a wok – although it does help – I find a good quality large frying pan heated with oil until it is almost at smoking point cooks any stir-fry dish to perfection.

1 Heat the oil in a large frying pan or wok and add the onion and garlic. Cook over high heat for 5 minutes until softened.

2 Add the peppers, baby corn, courgette, mangetout and mushrooms and stir-fry for 5 minutes until the vegetables are just softened and begin to turn brown. Stir the mixture frequently to prevent the vegetables sticking to the base of the pan and burning.

3 Meanwhile, stir-fry or boil the noodles in a separate saucepan, according to the packet instructions. Once cooked, stir the plum sauce into the noodles and serve with the stir-fried vegetables.

2 tablespoons rosemary or olive oil

1 large onion, peeled and sliced

2 cloves garlic, peeled and finely chopped

1 red pepper, deseeded and sliced

1 green pepper, deseeded and sliced

1 orange pepper, deseeded and sliced

125 g baby corn, trimmed and halved

1 medium courgette, cut into thick strips

125 g mangetout, halved

150 g enoki mushrooms, trimmed

250 g dried Oriental noodles

4 tablespoons plum sauce

Serves 4 (or 6–8 as a side dish)

CHICKEN AND SUMMER VEGETABLE STIR-FRY

Slice 4 skinned and boned chicken breasts into fine strips. Heat 2 tablespoons of olive oil in a large frying pan or wok and add the chicken strips. Stir-fry over high heat for 5 minutes, until the chicken turns golden brown.

Add 4 sliced spring onions, 2 crushed garlic cloves, 1 green and 1 yellow pepper, deseeded and sliced, 350 g of baby carrots, halved lengthways and 225 g of trimmed French beans to the pan. Stir-fry for 8 minutes. Finally, add 2 tablespoons of soy sauce and season with black pepper. Serve this stir-fry with plain boiled rice or noodles.

DUCK AND SUMMER VEGETABLE STIR-FRY

Slice 4 skinned and boned duck fillets into fine strips. Heat 2 tablespoons of olive oil in a large frying pan and add the strips of duck. Cook over high heat for 4–5 minutes until the duck is brown on the outside but remains slightly pink in the middle. Then add the prepared vegetables as for Chicken and Summer Vegetable Stir-fry and cook as instructed above.

STIR-FRY TIPS

A stir-fry is, essentially, cooked rapidly, so it is vital when making it to prepare all the ingredients in advance, so that they are ready to throw into the pan when required. Vegetables and meat should be cut into strips.

For best results, and to ensure that the meat and vegetables are cooked quickly, the oil should be almost smoking before any of the ingredients are added to the pan.

It is advisable to stir the mixture constantly during cooking to ensure that each component of the stir-fry is evenly cooked and does not burn or stick.

4

Vegetable & Side Dishes

POTATOES

MIXED VEGETABLES

TOMATOES

SAUCES & STOCKS

CURRIED SWEET POTATO

680 g sweet potatoes, peeled and cubed

4 tablespoons olive oil

1 teaspoon crushed dried chilli

1 tablespoon garam masala

150 ml vegetable stock (see page 77)

Serves 6

The pleasing sweetness of this brightly coloured vegetable marries surprisingly well with the flavours of chilli and garam masala, to produce a sweet and spicy side dish (see above).

1 Place the cubed potatoes in a large saucepan, cover with cold water and bring to a boil. Reduce the heat and simmer for 5 minutes. Then drain and set aside.

2 Heat the oil in a large frying pan that has a lid and add the chilli and garam masala. Cook over medium heat for 2 minutes, stirring constantly until the spices are well blended with the oil.

3 Add the potatoes to the pan and stir well so the spices and oil coat each piece of potato. Then add the vegetable stock and bring the liquid to a boil, stirring constantly.

4 Reduce the heat and simmer covered for 15 minutes, stirring occasionally until the potatoes are tender. Remove the potatoes from the pan and place them on a warmed serving dish. Serve with chicken, prawn or lamb curry.

SEARED NEW POTATOES WITH ROSEMARY & SEA SALT

New potatoes are perfect for frying. To give them additional flavour and a wonderful fragrance, cook them in olive oil with a few sprigs of rosemary. When buying new potatoes, ensure the skin rubs away easily and select the smallest ones in order to speed up the cooking time.

4 tablespoons extra virgin olive oil

900 g new potatoes, washed

1 teaspoon sea salt

Black pepper to taste

6 sprigs fresh rosemary

Serves 4–6

1 Pour the olive oil into a large heavy-based saucepan that has a lid and cook over high heat until sizzling. Add the potatoes and salt to the hot oil – do this carefully because the oil is likely to spit as you add the salt. Cover the pan with a lid and cook the potatoes for 10 minutes, shaking the pan frequently to prevent them scorching.

2 Add the black pepper and rosemary and stir well to coat the potatoes. Cover the pan again and cook for a further 5–10 minutes. Stir the potatoes several times during cooking to ensure they do not burn. Remove them from the pan and place them in a warmed serving bowl. These potatoes are delicious served with Poached Salmon (see page 44), Herb-coated Turkey (see page 28) and Poussin with Sticky Glaze (see page 53).

POTATO CAKES

Potato Cakes are quick and easy to prepare and are highly versatile – use them as an alternative to a side dish of boiled potatoes or, for a special treat, serve them for breakfast with poached eggs.

680 g potatoes, peeled

3 spring onions, washed and trimmed

1 egg, medium-sized

2 teaspoons wholegrain mustard

Salt and black pepper to taste

2 tablespoons olive oil

Serves 4

1 Grate the potatoes on to a sheet of kitchen paper and pat dry. Then place into a large mixing bowl.

2 Finely slice the onions and stir them into the grated potato. Stir in the egg and mustard. Season with salt and black pepper.

3 Heat the oil in a large frying pan over high heat. Take a tablespoon of the potato mixture and, using a second spoon, push the mixture off the first spoon into the hot oil. Repeat until the frying pan is full. Cook the potato cakes for 4–5 minutes on each side until browned and cooked through. Remove from the pan and place on kitchen paper to absorb any excess oil. Keep this first batch warm while frying the second batch in the same way.

Perfect Jacket Potatoes

4 baking potatoes (each weighing approximately 180 g)

Coarse sea salt to taste

2 tablespoons sesame oil

Serves 4

It is surprisingly simple to cook a jacket potato badly – with rubbery skin and dried-out flesh. But it is also easy to do it well. The best way to come up trumps every time – with crispy skins and soft flesh – is to coat the potatoes in sesame oil, sprinkle them with sea salt and bake them in a hot oven for one hour. You can then stuff them using any of the fillings below (each recipe fills four potatoes) and serve them on their own or with a selection of cold meats or smoked fish.

1 Preheat the oven to 200°C, gas mark 6. Wash the potatoes and prick them in several places with a fork. Pat them dry with kitchen paper.

2 Sit the potatoes in a roasting tin and sprinkle with sea salt. Drizzle the sesame oil over the potatoes and bake in the preheated oven for 1 hour, until the skins are dark and crispy. Use a fork or a table knife to pierce the potatoes – if the flesh is soft, the potatoes are cooked through.

3 Remove the potatoes from the tin and place on serving plates. To fill them, cut halfway into each potato using a sharp knife and gently press the potatoes open with your fingers. Spoon your chosen filling (see below) into the opened-out potato and serve immediately.

BACON, OLIVE AND SPINACH FILLING

Chop 150 g of back bacon into small pieces. Place in a frying pan and cook over low heat until the fat begins to run. Add 75 g of pitted and halved black olives, and 50 g of trimmed young spinach leaves to the pan and continue to cook for 2–3 minutes until the spinach just begins to wilt. Remove from the pan and carefully spoon the mixture into the potatoes to serve.

AVOCADO AND PRAWN FILLING

Peel, stone and chop 1 large avocado and place the flesh in a bowl. Stir in the grated rind and juice of 1 lime, taking care not to mash the avocado flesh. Then add 250 g of cooked prawns and season with plenty of black pepper. Spoon the mixture into the potatoes to serve.

TOMATO AND SMOKED TOFU FILLING

Heat 2 tablespoons of oil in a saucepan and add 1 peeled and chopped onion and 2 peeled and crushed cloves of garlic. Cook over medium heat until soft. Add 420 g of canned chopped tomatoes and 250 g of cubed smoked tofu. Cook over high heat until the mixture thickens. Stir in 2 tablespoons of chopped fresh coriander, season with salt and black pepper and spoon into the potatoes.

BEEF AND HORSERADISH FILLING

Scoop the potato flesh out of the potato skins using a spoon. Place the skins in the oven to keep warm. Beat the potato flesh with 3 tablespoons of grated horseradish in a bowl. Fold in 300 g of cubed corned beef and 2 tablespoons of snipped fresh chives. Spoon the mixture into the potato skins and serve.

COURGETTES WITH RED PEPPER, GARLIC & ROSEMARY

2 tablespoons olive oil

1 red pepper, deseeded and sliced

900 g courgettes, trimmed and sliced

3 cloves garlic, peeled and sliced

8 sprigs fresh rosemary

Salt and black pepper to taste

Serves 4

This colourful vegetable stir-fry is very quick to prepare and the wonderfully fragrant flavours of garlic and rosemary marry well with the sweet red pepper and courgettes.

1. Heat the oil in a large frying pan and add the red pepper. Cook over high heat for 5 minutes until the pepper begins to soften.

2. Add the courgettes and garlic. Continue to stir-fry over high heat for a further 6 minutes until the courgettes and peppers become tender and begin to brown.

3. Add the rosemary sprigs and season with salt and black pepper. Cook for a further 2 minutes, stirring constantly. Serve the vegetables hot with roast meats or steamed fish.

ORANGE-GLAZED BABY CARROTS

500 g baby carrots, trimmed

1 tablespoon coriander seeds

80 ml orange juice

Salt to taste

Serves 4

The secret to this recipe is to cook the carrots very gently in order to retain their natural sweetness – doing so in orange juice enhances their flavour. With baby carrots, you should remove the shoots as soon as possible, as these rob the carrots of their moisture and goodness.

1. Gently remove any dirt from the carrots and rinse under running cold water. Place in a large mixing bowl.

2. Stir the coriander seeds and orange juice into the carrots and mix well. Season with salt.

3. Place the mixture in a large saucepan and cook over low heat for 8 minutes until the carrots are tender and the juice reduces to a sticky glaze. Serve with roast spring lamb.

ORANGE-GLAZED SWEET POTATOES AND PARSNIPS

As with baby carrots, sweet potatoes and parsnips have a wonderfully sweet taste that works well with the flavour of oranges.

Peel and cube 250 g each of sweet potatoes and parsnips and place them in a large mixing bowl. Stir in 80 ml of orange juice and 1 tablespoon of fenugreek seeds in place of the coriander seeds and mix well until the vegetables are well coated. Season with salt to taste and place the mixture in a large saucepan. Cook for 12–15 minutes until the vegetables are soft. Serve with roast beef.

PUMPKIN WITH CARAWAY SEEDS

In this recipe, the addition of caraway seeds adds a nutty, aromatic taste to the mild and sweet flavour of roasted pumpkins. The pumpkin flesh is shaped with a melon baller, but if you find the flesh is too firm, simply cut it into cubes using a knife. Pumpkins are in season in the autumn and winter – always choose those that are free from skin blemishes and seem heavy for their size.

550 g pumpkin flesh, skinned and deseeded

85 ml white vegetable fat

2 tablespoons caraway seeds, toasted

Salt and black pepper to taste

Serves 4

1   Preheat the oven to 220°C, gas mark 7. Shape the pumpkin flesh into balls using a melon baller, or chop it into cubes using a knife if it is too firm.

2   Heat the fat in a small roasting tin on the hob until sizzling. Carefully add the pumpkin balls and stir well to coat them thoroughly in the fat. Roast in the preheated oven for 30 minutes until the pumpkin is just tender and lightly browned.

3   Place a heavy-based frying pan over high heat for 1 minute. Reduce the heat and add the caraway seeds. Cook over low heat for 1–2 minutes, stirring occasionally until the seeds are well toasted, then set aside.

4   Drain the pumpkin balls, place them in a serving bowl with the toasted caraway seeds and stir to mix the ingredients thoroughly. Season with salt and black pepper. Serve hot with roast pork.

PATTY PAN RISOTTO

Patty pans are miniature squash that are either bright yellow or green in colour. They are delicious steamed, fried or cooked with rice, as in this delicious vegetarian dish. The best thing about this particular risotto recipe is that it is made in the oven so there is no need to stand by the cooker stirring it all the time!

2 tablespoons olive oil

4 spring onions, peeled and chopped

2 cloves garlic, peeled and crushed

350 g Arborio risotto rice

900 ml vegetable stock (see page 77)

Black pepper to taste

450 g green and yellow patty pans, peeled, trimmed and quartered

Freshly grated soya cheese to serve (optional)

Serves 4 (or 2 as a main course)

1   Preheat the oven to 220°C, gas mark 7. Place the oil, spring onions and garlic into a large roasting tin and place on the floor of the oven. Cook for 5 minutes until the onions are soft.

2   Remove the tin from the oven and add the rice. Stir well to coat all the grains thoroughly in the oil. Stir in the stock and return the tin to the floor of the oven. Cook for a further 20 minutes.

3   Remove the tin from the oven and add the black pepper and patty pans to the rice mixture. Stir to combine all the ingredients. Cover the tin with foil and return it to the floor of the oven. Cook for a further 20 minutes until the rice is tender and it has absorbed the stock completely and the patty pans are cooked. Serve sprinkled with soya cheese, if desired.

Mediterranean Stuffed Aubergine

4 aubergines, medium-sized
(each weighing approximately 350 g)

2 tablespoons extra virgin olive oil

4 spring onions, trimmed and sliced

2 cloves garlic, peeled and
finely chopped

2 large peppers, I yellow and I green,
deseeded and chopped

4 ripe tomatoes, quartered and deseeded

2 tablespoons dried oregano

Salt and black pepper to taste

Fresh oregano leaves to garnish

Serves 8 (or 4 as a main course)

Aubergines filled with a colourful mix of peppers, tomatoes, onions and herbs are a perfect light meal for non-meat eaters (see below) as well as a substantial vegetable side dish, ideal with grilled meats and fish.

1 Preheat the oven to 200°C, gas mark 6. Cut each of the aubergines in half lengthways, then carefully scoop out the flesh from each aubergine using a spoon, leaving the skin (and a layer of flesh to reinforce the skin) as a case. Lightly brush the inside and outside of each case with some of the olive oil, then set the skins aside.

2 Cut the aubergine flesh into chunks. Heat the remaining oil in a large frying pan and add the aubergine flesh, spring onions and garlic. Cook over high heat for 3 minutes until the vegetables are soft.

3 Add the chopped peppers and the tomatoes to the pan with the aubergine and onion and continue to cook for a further 5 minutes until the vegetables begin to brown. Stir in the dried oregano and season the mixture with salt and black pepper.

4 Arrange the aubergine cases side-by-side on a large baking sheet and fill them with the cooked vegetable mixture.

5 Bake in the preheated oven for 15 minutes, until the aubergine cases are cooked through, but still hold their shape and the vegetable fillings are piping hot. To serve, garnish with the oregano leaves.

AUBERGINE CAVIAR

Preheat the oven to 200°C, gas mark 6. Cut 3 medium-sized aubergines (each weighing approximately 350 g) in half and score the flesh with a knife. Place in a roasting tin and cook in the preheated oven for 25 minutes until soft and cooked through.

Scoop the flesh out of the cooked aubergines using a metal spoon and place in a food processor. Blend with 2 cloves of garlic and 6 tablespoons of olive oil. (Alternatively, mash the flesh in a mixing bowl with a potato masher and mix in the garlic, then gradually blend in the oil.) Season with salt and black pepper to taste and serve on toast or as a dip with vegetable crudités.

GNOCCHI-TOPPED VEGETABLES

Gnocchi are small Italian dumplings made from flour, semolina and potato starch. (Do check the label if using shop-bought gnocchi since many varieties contain skimmed milk.) Gnocchi are certainly very versatile – they can be baked, steamed or fried – and combined with a whole host of savoury sauces. In this recipe, I have used them as a quick and simple topping to a robust and tasty vegetable mixture.

FOR THE VEGETABLES

2 tablespoons olive oil

1 onion, peeled and chopped

2 cloves garlic, peeled and crushed

2 large peppers, 1 red and 1 green, deseeded and chopped

2 courgettes, medium-sized, halved and sliced

400 g canned chopped tomatoes

Salt and black pepper to taste

FOR THE TOPPING

400 g fresh gnocchi

2 tablespoons olive oil

Serves 4 (or 2 as a main course)

1 Preheat the oven to 200°C, gas mark 6. To prepare the vegetables, heat the oil in a large frying pan and add the onion. Cook over medium heat until softened, not browned. Add the garlic, peppers and courgettes and cook for a further 5 minutes, stirring occasionally.

2 Add the canned tomatoes and bring to a boil. Reduce the heat and simmer uncovered for 5 minutes. Season with salt and black pepper.

3 To prepare the topping, place the gnocchi in a large saucepan of boiling salted water and cook over medium heat for 2–3 minutes, or according to the packet instructions. Drain the gnocchi thoroughly.

4 Spoon the vegetable mixture into a medium-sized ovenproof dish and top with the gnocchi. Sprinkle olive oil over the gnocchi. Bake in the oven for 25 minutes until the topping is golden brown. Serve hot as an accompaniment to a lamb or pork dish or as a vegetarian main course.

FENNEL & MANGETOUT STIR-FRY

2 tablespoons groundnut oil

1 bulb fennel, thinly sliced and shredded

3 spring onions, trimmed and halved

150 g trimmed mangetout, halved lengthways

150 g enoki mushrooms, trimmed

4 tablespoons light soy sauce

50 g cashew nuts, toasted and coarsely chopped

Salt and black pepper to taste

Serves 6

The anise-like flavour of fennel complements the subtle sweetness of mangetout in this dish that is excellent served with grilled fish.

1 Heat the groundnut oil in a wok or large frying pan and add the fennel and spring onions. Stir-fry for 3 minutes, stirring constantly. Add the mangetout and mushrooms and continue to stir-fry for a further 3 minutes.

2 Keeping the pan on the heat, stir in the soy sauce and cashew nuts and season with salt and black pepper. Serve the stir-fry with grilled fish and plain boiled rice or noodles.

CELERY AND SUGAR SNAP PEA STIR-FRY

For a more subtle flavour, replace the fennel with 1 head of celery, thinly sliced. Replace the mangetout with sugar snap peas and the enoki mushrooms with 150 g of trimmed and halved button mushrooms.

VEGETARIAN STUFFED CABBAGE

1 savoy cabbage (weighing approximately 680 g)

1 tablespoon olive oil

1 red onion, peeled and chopped

50 g pine nuts, toasted

3 tablespoons plain soya yogurt

Salt and black pepper to taste

600 ml vegetable stock (see page 77)

4 sprigs fresh marjoram

6 peppercorns

Serves 4

Cabbage parcels bulging with onions and nuts are a warming dish and ideal served with fresh Tomato Sauce (see page 77). Choose a cabbage with crispy leaves that are firmly packed together.

1 Discard the outermost leaves of the cabbage. Break off the next 8 leaves and remove the core. Finely shred 50 g of the remaining cabbage and reserve. Immerse the 8 whole reserved leaves in a pan of boiling water for 1 minute, rinse with cold water and leave to drain.

2 Heat the oil in a large frying pan and add the onion. Cook over medium heat for 5 minutes until softened. Add the shredded cabbage and stir-fry for 2 minutes. Remove from the heat and stir in the pine nuts and yogurt. Season with salt and black pepper.

3 Lay the whole cabbage leaves on a work surface and divide the onion and pine nut filling between them. Fold the leaves over the filling to form a parcel and tie each one with string. Arrange the parcels in a single layer in a large saucepan.

4 Pour the stock over the parcels and add the marjoram and peppercorns. Bring the stock to a boil, then reduce the heat and simmer for 15 minutes. Drain the cooked cabbage parcels thoroughly, then remove the string. Place 2 parcels on each plate and serve with fresh Tomato Sauce (see page 77) or with grilled meat or fish.

RED CABBAGE WITH PEARS

For this colourful side dish (see above), red cabbage and pears are cooked gently in fruit juice to produce a deliciously sweet flavour. Serve as an accompaniment to roast meats or hearty winter stews.

1　Heat the oil over medium heat in a large heavy-based saucepan that has a lid. Add the bay leaves, juniper berries and onion. Cook for 5 minutes until the onion is softened, not browned.

2　Place the shredded red cabbage into the pan and stir until it is well coated in the oil and combined with the other ingredients. Cook over low heat for 15 minutes, stirring occasionally.

3　Add the pears, fruit juice and sugar to the pan. Stir the mixture thoroughly to combine with the other ingredients and cover. Simmer over low heat for a further 15 minutes, until the cabbage and fruit are soft. Season with salt and black pepper to serve.

1 tablespoon olive oil

2 bay leaves, lightly bruised

4 juniper berries, bruised

1 small onion, peeled and thinly sliced

450 g red cabbage, shredded

2 pears, peeled, cored and chopped

150 ml pear or apple juice

3 tablespoons soft light brown sugar

Salt and black pepper to taste

Serves 4

ROAST TOMATOES WITH BALSAMIC VINEGAR

Roasting plum tomatoes retains their fresh juiciness and full flavour. The exquisite taste of Italian balsamic vinegar sets off this dish to perfection. Serve the tomatoes with barbecued meats or roast poultry.

1 Preheat the oven to 220°C, gas mark 7. Arrange the onion slices in a medium-sized ovenproof dish or baking sheet.

2 Cut a thin slice from the base of each tomato so they can sit without rolling over. Make a few small slits in the skin of each tomato and press a slice of garlic into each one. Sit the tomatoes on top of the onion slices.

3 Push a sprig of rosemary into the top of each tomato, pushing it through to pierce the onion beneath. Drizzle with oil and sprinkle with salt, pepper and sugar. Roast in the oven for 20 minutes until the tomatoes are soft and cooked through. Serve immediately, drizzled with balsamic vinegar.

1 red onion, peeled and cut into 8 slices

8 plum tomatoes

2 cloves garlic, peeled and thinly sliced

8 sprigs fresh rosemary

4 tablespoons extra virgin olive oil

Course sea salt and cracked pepper to taste

2 teaspoons caster sugar

Balsamic vinegar to serve

Serves 4

ROAST BABY AUBERGINES

Baby aubergines can be cooked in the same way as the tomatoes above. Use 300 g of baby aubergines in place of the plum tomatoes and substitute sprigs of oregano for the rosemary. Make a hole in the top of each baby aubergine using a skewer to allow the oregano sprigs to pierce through to the onions.

TRIPLE TOMATO & AVOCADO SALAD

I have used three types of tomato in this refreshing salad – sweet red and yellow cherry tomatoes combine perfectly with the stronger flavour of sun-dried tomato paste to create a tasty filling for creamy avocados.

1 Halve and stone the avocados. Pour the lime juice over the flesh. Fill the hollow left by the stone with the mixed cherry tomatoes.

2 Place the sun-dried tomatoes in a food processor with the oil and honey. Blend until they are well combined. (Alternatively, crush the tomatoes in a mortar with a pestle and gradually mix in the oil and honey.) Season with salt and black pepper.

3 Spread a teaspoon of the tomato paste on to the tomato-filled avocados, arrange the rocket leaves over the top and serve.

2 ripe avocados

1 tablespoon lime juice

125 g each red and yellow cherry tomatoes, halved

3 sun-dried tomatoes

3 tablespoons olive oil

1 tablespoon clear honey

Salt and black pepper to taste

50 g baby rocket leaves

Serves 4

BASIC WHITE SAUCE

Dairy-free white sauce is wonderfully versatile and a good substitute for the traditional butter and milk-based version.

25 g non-dairy margarine

25 g cornflour

450 ml soya milk

Salt and black pepper to taste

Makes 500 ml

1 Place the margarine in a non-stick saucepan and melt it over medium heat. Remove the pan from the heat. Mix the cornflour with 3 tablespoons of the milk in a mixing bowl until smooth. Add to the pan and stir well.

2 Gradually add the remaining soya milk, stirring constantly to retain a smooth texture. Return the pan to the heat and bring slowly to a boil, stirring constantly until the sauce begins to thicken. Then, reduce the heat and simmer for 2 minutes until thick. Season with salt and black pepper.

FLAVOURINGS

A wide variety of flavourings can be added to Basic White Sauce mixture at the end of preparation. To serve with fish, stir in 2 tablespoons of chopped fresh mixed herbs such as dill, chervil or flat-leaf parsley. To serve with meat, stir in 2 tablespoons of chopped fresh mixed herbs such as thyme, parsley, sage or coriander. To serve with poultry, stir in 1 tablespoon of wholegrain mustard.

MAYONNAISE

This thick and 'creamy' mayonnaise is easy to prepare and delicious served with cold salads or hot fish and meat dishes.

1 egg, medium-sized

Large pinch of mustard powder

Salt and black pepper to taste

1 tablespoon white wine vinegar

150 ml olive oil

Makes 200 ml

1 Place the egg in a food processor with the mustard, seasoning and vinegar. Blend until all the ingredients are combined and the mixture is smooth.

2 With the motor still running, gradually add the oil, drop by drop, to form a thick and glossy mayonnaise.

HAND-MADE MAYONNAISE

Place 1 egg yolk in a mixing bowl and whisk in the mustard, seasoning and vinegar. Gradually add the oil, whisking continuously until the mixture becomes thick and glossy.

FLAVOURINGS

Various flavourings can be added to the basic mayonnaise mixture at the end of preparation. To serve with poultry, stir in 2 tablespoons of chopped fresh tarragon. To serve with fish, stir in either 2 tablespoons of chopped fresh dill or 2 tablespoons of finely chopped caperberries.

TOMATO SAUCE

A tomato-based sauce is one of the most useful recipes in a lactose-free diet as it can be used as a substitute for most creamy or cheese sauces and is delicious with pasta, vegetables, meat or fish dishes.

1   Heat the oil in a saucepan over medium heat and add the shallots and garlic. Cook them for 5 minutes, stirring occasionally to prevent them becoming browned.

2   Add the tomatoes and tomato purée to the pan and stir to mix all the ingredients. Slowly bring the mixture to a boil. Reduce the heat and simmer for 15 minutes until the tomatoes are soft and the sauce is thick. Stir in the chopped basil and season with salt and black pepper.

3 tablespoons olive oil

2 shallots, peeled and chopped

2 cloves garlic, peeled and chopped

1.5 kg ripe tomatoes, skinned, deseeded and chopped

2 tablespoons sun-dried tomato purée

3 tablespoons chopped fresh basil

Salt and black pepper to taste

Makes 900 ml

STOCKS

Stock can be refrigerated in a plastic container for three days or can be frozen (omitting the seasoning) in ice cube trays for up to two months.

FISH STOCK
Place 300 g of fish heads and bones in a large saucepan with 1 peeled and halved onion, a small bunch of fresh parsley stalks and 3 slices of lime. Cover with cold water and slowly bring to a boil. Skim the surface using a small sieve to remove any impurities, then reduce the heat and simmer for 10–15 minutes. Strain, discard the fish bones and onion and use the liquid as required.

CHICKEN STOCK
Place 400 g of chicken carcass in a saucepan with 100 g of chopped vegetables, such as carrots, celery and onions, 1 bouquet garni, 4 black peppercorns and 700 ml of cold water. Bring to a boil, then cover and simmer for 60–90 minutes, skimming the surface during cooking. Strain and use the liquid as required.

VEGETABLE STOCK
Place 450 g of chopped vegetables, such as leeks, onions, carrots and celery into a saucepan with 1.5 litres of cold water. Bring to a boil, then cover and simmer for 50 minutes. Strain, gently pressing the vegetables to extract all the flavour.

LAMB STOCK
Preheat the oven to 230°C, gas mark 8. Place 1 kg of lamb bones in a roasting tin and brown in the oven for 15 minutes. Add 1 chopped carrot, 1 chopped stick of celery and 1 chopped leek. Roast for a further 15 minutes, then transfer to a saucepan with 1.5 litres of cold water, 1 bouquet garni, 4 black peppercorns and 1 tablespoon of tomato purée. Bring to a boil, then cover and simmer for 2 hours, skimming the surface during cooking. Strain and use as required.

5

Food for Kids

Avocado & Tuna Stuffed Tomatoes

4 large tomatoes

2 ripe avocados, stoned, peeled and cut into chunks

Grated rind and juice of ½ lemon

2 spring onions, trimmed and sliced

200 g canned tuna chunks, drained

150 ml plain soya yogurt

Salt and black pepper to taste

4 slices bread

Fresh chives to garnish

Serves 4

A delicious mix of tuna chunks, avocados and soya yogurt is used to fill tomatoes in this attractive meal-in-one (see below), which tastes as good as it looks! The versatile filling can also be stirred into cooked, cooled pasta and served as a salad.

1 Slice the tops off the tomatoes and discard. Carefully scoop out the tomato seeds with a small metal spoon, leaving a tomato 'shell'.

2 Stir the avocado chunks and lemon juice together in a mixing bowl, taking care not to mash the avocados. Then fold in the lemon rind, spring onions, tuna chunks and yogurt. Season with salt and black pepper. Place the tomato shells on a chopping board and fill them carefully with the tuna and avocado mixture.

3 Cut the bread slices into circles slightly larger than the tomato shells and toast them under a hot grill for 1–2 minutes on both sides until lightly browned. Place one on each serving plate and sit the filled tomatoes on the top. Garnish with a few snipped chives and serve immediately.

BACON AND COUSCOUS STUFFED TOMATOES

Slice the tops off the tomatoes and scoop out the seeds as instructed in the recipe opposite. Chop 250 g of bacon into cubes.

Heat 1 tablespoon of olive oil in a frying pan and add the cubed bacon. Cook over high heat for 5 minutes until the bacon is fairly crispy, then add 125 g of diced courgette and cook for a further 5 minutes until the courgette begins to soften. Remove the bacon and courgette from the heat and set aside.

Prepare 125 g of couscous according to the packet instructions. Separate the grains with a fork, then mix in the bacon and courgette and stir until all the ingredients are combined. Season with salt and black pepper to taste. Spoon the mixture into the tomato shells, place on toasted bread circles and serve.

MUSHROOM AND TOFU STUFFED TOMATOES

Preheat the oven to 190°C, gas mark 5. Slice the tops off the tomatoes and scoop out the seeds as instructed in the recipe opposite.

Wash and slice 150 g of mixed mushrooms. Heat 1 tablespoon of olive oil in a frying pan and add the sliced mushrooms. Cook them over medium heat for 5 minutes until they begin to soften. Add 100 g of finely cubed tofu and cook for a further 3 minutes until the tofu is heated through. Finally, stir in 1 tablespoon of sesame seeds and mix well.

Spoon the mushroom and tofu mixture into the tomato shells and bake in the preheated oven for 10 minutes, until the tofu is cooked through. Serve hot, placed on toasted bread circles.

TOMATO CATHERINE WHEELS

Filo pastry is tightly rolled with a filling of sun-dried tomato paste. The rolls are then sliced to reveal a pretty spiral pattern. Tomato Catherine Wheels look lovely arranged on a platter and are the ideal snack for children's parties – the grown-ups like them too, with drinks. They also make a great substitute for croutons when served with soups.

50 g filo pastry, 3 sheets measuring approximately 40 x 30 cm

6 tablespoons sun-dried tomato paste

1 egg, beaten to glaze

Mayonnaise to serve (see page 76)

125 g cooked ham or chicken, chopped (optional)

Makes 20–25

1   Preheat the oven to 190°C, gas mark 5. Lay the sheets of filo pastry flat on a work surface. Spread each sheet with a thin layer of sun-dried tomato paste. Tightly roll up each sheet from the wider edge like a Swiss roll.

2   Cut each roll into 1 cm-thick slices using a sharp knife and place them on a large baking sheet. Brush the top of each slice with some beaten egg. Bake in the preheated oven for 8 minutes until the pastry is golden brown and cooked through and the filling is hot.

3   Place the filo rolls on to a large platter and serve with a dip of ready-made or home-made Mayonnaise (see page 76) in a separate bowl. If desired, these rolls can be topped with finely chopped ham or chicken.

FISH CAKES WITH TOMATO SALSA

FOR THE FISH CAKES

750 g large potatoes, peeled and chopped

750 g haddock fillet

4 black peppercorns

1 bay leaf

2 tablespoons chopped fresh chervil or parsley

Salt and black pepper to taste

2 eggs, medium-sized

150 g fresh white breadcrumbs

2 tablespoons olive oil

FOR THE TOMATO SALSA

4 medium-ripe tomatoes, deseeded and chopped

1 red pepper, deseeded and chopped

4 sticks celery, trimmed and chopped

2 tablespoons olive oil

Makes 12

My own children, Alicia and Sophie, love these haddock fish cakes which are served with a chunky tomato salsa (see right). In fact, they are so popular with the kids that I have deliberately increased the measures of the recipe in order to produce a large quantity of fish cakes, so that half can be enjoyed immediately while the rest can be frozen for another day. Allow 1–2 fish cakes per child.

1 To prepare the fish cakes, place the potatoes in a saucepan, cover with water and bring to a boil. Reduce the heat and simmer for 15 minutes until the potatoes are tender. Drain the potatoes, then mash until smooth.

2 Meanwhile, place the haddock fillet in a large shallow saucepan and add the peppercorns and bay leaf. Cover with boiling water and cook the fish over gentle heat for 5 minutes until the flesh flakes easily. Once cooked, drain the fish and discard the bones and skin.

3 Coarsely flake the fish and place it in a large bowl. Mix in the mashed potato and chervil or parsley and season with salt and black pepper. Mould the mixture into 12 round patties using lightly floured hands to prevent the potato and fish mixture from becoming sticky.

4 Place the breadcrumbs in a shallow container. Dip each fish cake first into the beaten egg and then into the breadcrumbs, turning them until they are evenly coated. Chill the fish cakes in the refrigerator for 30 minutes. Alternatively, wrap them in kitchen foil and freeze them at this point.

5 When ready to serve, heat the oil in a large frying pan and add the fish cakes. Cook over medium heat for 3–4 minutes on both sides until golden and cooked through. Do this in small batches, keeping the cooked fish cakes warm in the oven while cooking the next batch.

6 To prepare the tomato salsa, place the chopped tomatoes, pepper and celery in a bowl and mix together. Drizzle in the olive oil and stir until all the vegetables are coated in oil. Serve the fish cakes hot with the tomato salsa and a green salad.

COD FISH CAKES WITH CUCUMBER SALSA

A cod fillet may be used as a substitute for the haddock in the recipe above. Cod fish cakes work well with a cucumber salsa – replace the tomatoes in the salsa recipe with a 12 cm piece of deseeded and chopped cucumber.

Chicken Goujons & Chips

FOR THE CHICKEN GOUJONS

1 egg, medium-sized

½ teaspoon turmeric

25 g fresh wholemeal breadcrumbs

25 g oatmeal

2 chicken breasts, skinned and boned

3 tablespoons sunflower oil

FOR THE CHIPS

450 g large potatoes

Sunflower oil for frying

Coarse sea salt to taste

Serves 4 (makes 450 g)

Both the chicken goujons and the chips (see above) can be prepared up to four hours ahead of cooking: coat the chicken strips in breadcrumbs and chill in the refrigerator; slice the potatoes into matchsticks and leave in a saucepan covered with cold water.

1 Preheat the oven to 200°C, gas mark 6. To prepare the chicken goujons, beat the egg with the turmeric in a shallow bowl and set aside. Then mix together the breadcrumbs and oatmeal in a separate bowl and set aside.

2 Slice the chicken breasts very thinly using a sharp knife. Dip the chicken strips into the egg and turmeric mixture, turning them frequently to coat the chicken thoroughly. Then dip the chicken strips into the breadcrumbs and oatmeal mixture, turning until each piece is evenly coated.

3 Place the coated chicken on a baking sheet and drizzle over the sunflower oil. Bake in the preheated oven for 15 minutes until the chicken is crisp on the outside and cooked through.

4 To prepare the chips, cut the potatoes into long matchsticks. Rinse in cold water and pat dry with kitchen paper.

5 Heat the oil in a heavy-based pan or deep-fat fryer and add the matchstick potatoes. Cook over high heat for 2–3 minutes, in batches if necessary. Drain thoroughly on kitchen paper and serve the chips immediately with the chicken goujons and a dollop of mayonnaise.

BEEF MEATBALLS WITH GOOEY CENTRES

Kids of all ages love these delicious meatballs which are cooked in tomato sauce and contain a lovely surprise. If people proclaim that dairy-free cooking is unexciting, I serve this dish to prove them wrong!

1   To prepare the meatballs, heat the oil in a frying pan and add the onion and garlic. Cook over medium heat for 5 minutes until softened. Remove from the heat and leave to cool.

2   Mix the cooled onions into the minced beef in a bowl and add the parsley, salt and black pepper. Do this with your hands to ensure the ingredients are evenly mixed. Cut the cheese into 20 cubes and, using lightly floured or damp hands (to prevent the mixture becoming sticky), surround each cube of cheese with some minced beef and mould into 20 balls.

3   To prepare the sauce, heat the oil in a frying pan and add the onion. Cook over medium heat for 5 minutes until softened, not browned. Remove from the pan and set aside. Now cook the meatballs in batches in the same pan over high heat for 10 minutes until browned. Remove and set aside.

4   Return the onions to the pan with the passatta and bring to a boil. Add the meatballs and simmer for 10 minutes until heated through. Season with salt and black pepper and serve with boiled rice and peas.

FOR THE MEATBALLS

2 tablespoons sunflower oil

1 onion, peeled and finely chopped

1 clove garlic, peeled and crushed

650 g minced beef

2 tablespoons chopped fresh parsley

Salt and black pepper to taste

25 g soya cheese

FOR THE SAUCE

1 tablespoon sunflower oil

1 onion, peeled and finely chopped

300 ml passatta

Salt and black pepper to taste

Serves 4

POLENTA-TOPPED PIE

Polenta is the staple carbohydrate of northern Italy. It can be cooked in many ways – here, it tastes great as a topping for minced beef.

1   Preheat the oven to 190°C, gas mark 5. Heat the olive oil in a large frying pan and add the onion and garlic. Cook over medium heat for 5 minutes until softened, not browned. Then stir in the minced beef and cook for 10–15 minutes until browned, stirring frequently to prevent it sticking to the base of the pan.

2   Stir in the chopped tomatoes, passatta and stock and then bring to a boil, stirring occasionally. Then simmer for 15 minutes until the meat is cooked through. Add the parsley and season with salt and black pepper.

3   Cook the polenta according to the packet instructions. Season with salt and black pepper. Spoon the beef mixture into a large ovenproof dish, top with the polenta mixture and smooth out the surface. Bake in the preheated oven for 25 minutes until the top is golden brown. Remove the pie from the oven and serve immediately with steamed broccoli.

1 tablespoon olive oil

1 large onion, peeled and finely chopped

2 cloves garlic, peeled and chopped

1 kg lean minced beef

420 g canned chopped tomatoes

150 ml passatta

150 ml beef stock

1 teaspoon dried parsley

Salt and black pepper to taste

180 g instant polenta

Serves 6

SPAGHETTI CARBONARA

I egg, medium-sized

4 teaspoons plain flour

200 ml plain soya yogurt

I tablespoon olive oil

I clove garlic, peeled and chopped

I onion, peeled and chopped

250 g trimmed back bacon, chopped

250 g dried spaghetti or pasta shapes

Salt and black pepper to taste

2 tablespoons chopped fresh
flat-leaf parsley

Serves 4

This popular Italian dish is traditionally made with a sauce of cream, eggs, Parmesan cheese and bacon. This lactose-free version uses flour and yogurt in place of the cream and cheese, and is just as tasty (see right). Add cooked fresh green peas to the spaghetti with the bacon and onions for extra colour if desired.

1 Beat the egg and flour together in a bowl until smooth. Gradually stir in the yogurt and set aside.

2 Heat the oil in a large frying pan and add the garlic and onion. Cook over medium heat until they soften and begin to brown. Add the bacon and continue to cook for 5 minutes until the bacon begins to brown.

3 Meanwhile, bring a large saucepan of lightly salted water to a boil. Add the dried spaghetti and cook according to packet instructions. Drain the spaghetti and place it back into the pan to keep hot.

4 Add the bacon and onion mixture and the egg and yogurt mixture to the hot spaghetti and mix well. Season with salt and black pepper and serve sprinkled with parsley.

HAM & EGG PARCELS

2 eggs, medium-sized

250 g filo pastry, 12–16 sheets measuring
approximately 40 x 30 cm

I tablespoon sunflower oil

300 g cooked ham, cubed

2 tablespoons plain soya yogurt

2 tablespoons snipped fresh chives

I egg, beaten, to glaze

Serves 8

Ham and eggs make a wonderful combination and they are especially delicious wrapped in filo pastry and then baked. For a more exotic filo parcel, replace the ham with the same quantity of cooked prawns.

1 Preheat the oven to 220°C, gas mark 7. Bring a small pan of water to a boil and add the eggs. Reduce the heat and simmer for 6–10 minutes. Remove the eggs and leave them under cold running water to cool. When cool enough to handle, peel and quarter them and set aside.

2 Layer 3–4 sheets of filo pastry, brushing each layer with oil before adding the next so that the sheets stick together. When you have 4 rectangles of layered pastry sheets, cut the rectangles in half to leave 8 squares. Divide the cubed ham into 8 and place 1 portion on each square with a quarter of hard-boiled egg. Make sure you place this filling in the middle of each square, leaving enough of the edges free to be folded over the mixture.

3 Mix together the yogurt and chives in a bowl and place a dollop of this mixture on top of the ham and egg. Brush a little of the beaten egg around the edge of the pastry. Fold the edges of the pastry over the filling to make parcels. Arrange the parcels on a baking sheet, brush them with beaten egg and bake in the preheated oven for 5–8 minutes until golden brown. Serve with a green salad.

Pork & Apple Burgers

A platter of these tempting mini burgers (see left) – made with a blend of pork, apples and mushrooms – always goes down well at children's parties. To freeze these burgers, prepare and shape them as described, then open-freeze them on sheets of clingfilm. Once frozen, transfer them to a rigid container. When ready to use, allow them to thaw completely on a wire rack for at least two hours, then cook as described below.

500 g minced pork

2 eating apples, cored and grated

125 g button mushrooms, finely chopped

Salt and black pepper to taste

2 tablespoons olive oil

20 mini bread rolls, halved

Tomato Relish to serve (see below)

3 little gem lettuces, washed and chopped

Serves 10

1 Mix together the minced pork, grated apple and chopped mushrooms in a large mixing bowl and season with plenty of salt and black pepper. Blend well, using your hands if necessary, to ensure that all the ingredients are thoroughly combined.

2 Divide the pork mixture into 20 portions and mould them into even-sized patties with lightly floured or dampened hands (to prevent the mixture becoming sticky). Place the burgers in a shallow dish, cover with clingfilm and chill in the refrigerator for 30 minutes or freeze as described above.

3 Heat the oil in a large frying pan and add the mini burgers. Cook over high heat for 5 minutes on each side until browned and cooked through. Do this in batches if necessary.

4 Cut the bread rolls in half and arrange the bases on a large serving plate. Spread half a teaspoon of Tomato Relish (see below) on each roll and then add a cooked burger. Place the other half of the roll over the top of the burger with some chopped lettuce and serve.

VEGETARIAN BURGERS

Replace the minced pork with 500 g of quorn and replace the eating apples with 3 finely sliced spring onions. Use these ingredients and prepare the burgers as described in the recipe above.

TOMATO RELISH

Peel, deseed and chop 500 g of ripe tomatoes. Heat 1 tablespoon of olive oil in a saucepan and add the tomatoes with 1 chopped stick of celery and 2 peeled and chopped shallots. Cook the vegetables over medium heat for 10 minutes until softened. Leave to cool before serving.

PIZZA WITH PORK & SWEETCORN

These mini pizzas topped with fresh tomato sauce, succulent pork and vegetables are marvellous for children's suppers. Pittas contain no dairy products, so make the perfect cheats' pizza base!

1 Preheat the oven to 200°C, gas mark 6. Arrange the mini pittas side-by-side on a large baking sheet.

2 Heat 2 tablespoons of the oil in a saucepan and add the onion and garlic. Cook over high heat until the onion is softened, not browned.

3 Add the tomatoes to the pan and stir well. Increase the heat and bring the mixture to a boil. Continue to boil for 10 minutes until the tomato sauce is thick, stirring frequently to prevent the mixture sticking to the base of the pan. Season with salt and black pepper.

4 Heat the remaining oil in a separate frying pan and add the chopped pork fillet. Cook over medium heat for 8–10 minutes, stirring frequently until the pork is browned and cooked through.

5 Spread the tomato sauce on the pittas and arrange the cooked pork, sliced pepper and the sweetcorn kernels on top. Bake in the preheated oven for 8–10 minutes until the topping is piping hot and the pittas are browned around the edges.

4 mini pittas

4 tablespoons sunflower oil

1 onion, peeled and chopped

2 cloves garlic, peeled and crushed

410 g canned chopped tomatoes

Salt and black pepper to taste

150 g pork fillets, roughly chopped

1 green pepper, deseeded and sliced

50 g sweetcorn kernels

Serves 4

HONEY SAUSAGES & MASH

Sausages roasted with honey and shallots and served with rich mash make the perfect winter warmer for your kids. Or sprinkle the sausages with toasted sesame seeds and watch them disappear at a drinks party.

1 Preheat the oven to 200°C, gas mark 6. To prepare the sausages, place them in a large roasting tin with the shallots. Drizzle the honey over the top and stir until the sausages and onions are well coated.

2 Place the tin in the preheated oven and roast the sausages and shallots for 20 minutes until 'sticky', golden and cooked through. Stir the mixture once or twice during cooking to ensure the sausages cook evenly and remain coated in honey.

3 Place the potatoes in a large saucepan and cover with cold water. Bring to a boil, reduce the heat and simmer for 15 minutes until soft. Drain, return to the pan and mash with the oil until smooth. Stir in the parsley and season with salt and black pepper. Serve immediately with the sausages.

FOR THE SAUSAGES

12 cocktail sausages

2 shallots, peeled and sliced into rings

85 ml clear honey

FOR THE MASH

300 g potatoes, peeled and chopped

2 tablespoons olive oil

2 tablespoons chopped fresh parsley

Salt and black pepper to serve

Serves 4

BAKED MARMALADE STEAMED PUDDINGS

Individual steamed puddings are baked in a bain-marie (a hot water bath) in this recipe, making them very light and fluffy. Grapefruit marmalade is used for the topping but you could also try fruit jams.

FOR THE PUDDINGS

Sunflower or groundnut oil for greasing

175 g non-dairy margarine

150 g demerara sugar

3 eggs, medium-sized

85 g ground almonds, sifted

125 g self-raising flour, sifted

6 tablespoons grapefruit marmalade

1 teaspoon freshly ground cardamom seeds

1 Preheat the oven to 190°C, gas mark 5. Grease 6 individual 175 ml pudding moulds with sunflower or groundnut oil.

2 Beat together the margarine and the demerara sugar in a bowl until light and fluffy. Beat in the eggs, then fold in the sifted almonds and flour.

3 Place 1 tablespoon of grapefruit marmalade in the base of each pudding mould. Pour over the sponge mixture and sprinkle the top with cardamom seeds. Place the moulds in a roasting tin that is half filled with boiling water. Bake for 25 minutes until risen and golden.

4　To prepare the orange glaze, place the caster sugar in a small saucepan. Carefully peel the oranges, holding them over the pan as you peel to catch any juice. Segment the oranges and set aside. Add 90 ml of cold water to the pan and heat gently until the sugar dissolves. Bring to a boil, then reduce the heat and simmer for 5 minutes. Add the orange segments and heat for a further 2 minutes.

5　Remove the puddings from the oven. Then run a sharp knife between the puddings and the moulds (if necessary) and carefully turn them out on to serving plates. Drizzle with the hot orange glaze to serve.

FOR THE ORANGE GLAZE

125 g caster sugar

3 oranges, peeled

Makes **6**

Chocolate Bread Pudding

This dairy-free version of Bread and Butter Pudding uses slices of Cinnamon Swirl Loaf and home-made Chocolate Sauce.

1　Place a roasting tin, half filled with water, in the oven and preheat the oven to 180°C, gas mark 4. Grease a 900 ml baking dish with oil.

2　Spread the slices of Cinnamon Swirl Loaf (see page 118) with margarine and cut into triangles. Arrange in the prepared dish, buttered-side-up, overlapping if necessary. Pour over the Chocolate Sauce (see page 97) and press the loaf down gently. Leave to stand for 15 minutes.

3　Sprinkle the pudding with sugar and place the dish in the tin containing the hot water. Bake in the oven for 25 minutes until the sauce has just set.

Oil for greasing

8 slices Cinnamon Swirl Loaf (see page 118) or fruit loaf

50 g non-dairy margarine for spreading

250 ml Chocolate Sauce (see page 97)

2 tablespoons demerara sugar

Serves **4**

Flapjacks

These fruity and nutritious biscuits are bursting with oats, nuts and dried fruit. They are easy to make and perfect for packed lunches.

1　Preheat the oven to 170°C, gas mark 3. Grease a 20.5 cm square tin with oil and line it with greaseproof paper.

2　Place the margarine and brown sugar in a saucepan and heat gently until the margarine melts and the sugar dissolves – be careful not to burn the mixture. Add the oats, walnut pieces, raisins and dried apricots and stir until all the ingredients are combined. Press the mixture into the tin.

3　Bake the mixture in the preheated oven for 40 minutes until golden. Remove from the oven and leave to cool for 5 minutes, then mark into squares. Leave the flapjacks in the tin to cool and set. Once cool, separate the squares and store them in an airtight container for 4 days or freeze for up to 1 month and thaw for 3 hours on a wire rack before serving.

Oil for greasing

175 g non-dairy margarine

175 g soft light brown sugar

350 g rolled porridge oats

50 g walnut pieces

50 g raisins

50 g ready-to-eat apricots, chopped

Makes **16 squares**

MINI PLUM CRUMBLES

These crumbles combine juicy cooked plums with an oaty crumble topping and are made in individual ramekins, which is the perfect amount for a child. They can also be frozen, uncooked, for one month.

1 Preheat the oven to 190°C, gas mark 5. To prepare the filling, place the plums and sugar in a large saucepan and heat gently for 10 minutes until the sugar dissolves and the fruit is soft.

2 To prepare the crumble topping, mix the flour and oatmeal together in a bowl. Rub in the margarine with your fingertips until the mixture resembles fine breadcrumbs. Then stir in the brown sugar.

3 Divide the filling between 6 individual 50 ml ramekins (or 1 large 900 ml dish) and top with the crumble mixture. Bake in the preheated oven for 20–25 minutes (15–20 minutes for 1 large crumble) and serve immediately.

FOR THE FILLING

680 g plums, stoned and quartered

100 g soft light brown sugar

FOR THE CRUMBLE TOPPING

150 g plain flour

25 g oatmeal

75 g non-dairy margarine

75 g soft light brown sugar

Serves 6

FRUITY MILK SHAKES

Soya milk, yogurt and red berries are blended to create these nutritious fruity shakes. Fresh or frozen raspberries or strawberries are the best berries to use as they give delicious flavour and vivid colour (see left).

Place the fruit and icing sugar in a food processor. Blend until a purée is formed then, with the motor still running, add the soya milk and yogurt. (Alternatively, pass the fruits through a sieve to purée and whisk in the soya milk and yogurt.) Divide the mixture between 2 tall glasses and add the crushed ice to serve.

250 g red berries

2 tablespoons icing sugar

250 ml soya milk or oat milk

250 ml plain soya yogurt

8 ice cubes, crushed

Makes 2

CHOCOLATE CHIP MUFFINS

Chocolate chip muffins (see left) make an ideal snack for children and adults alike. Ring the changes by adding chopped dried mango, sultanas or toasted hazelnuts in place of the chocolate chips.

1 Preheat the oven to 220°C, gas mark 7. Line 100 ml mini patty tins with mini paper muffin cases.

2 Sift together the flour, baking powder and caster sugar in a bowl. Beat together the egg, oat milk and cooled margarine in a separate bowl and stir into the flour mixture with the chocolate chips until well combined.

3 Spoon into the paper cases and bake in the oven for 15 minutes until risen and golden brown. Serve warm.

175 g self-raising flour

1 teaspoon baking powder

80 g caster sugar

1 egg, medium-sized

175 ml oat milk

125 g sunflower margarine, melted

125 g plain chocolate chips

Makes 30

6 Desserts

BLUEBERRY RICE PUDDING

50 g short-grain or pudding rice

25 g caster sugar

800 ml coconut milk

125 g dried blueberries or
250 g fresh blueberries

4 tablespoons plain soya yogurt

Dried coconut shreds to serve

Serves 4

Dried blueberries give this creamy rice pudding its striking purple colour (see above). For an equally delicious alternative, use dried cranberries, but add extra sugar or a few raisins to sweeten the dish.

1   Place the rice and sugar in a large saucepan and mix well to combine. Stir in the coconut milk and heat gently for 3–4 minutes, stirring occasionally until the sugar dissolves.

2   Add the blueberries and continue to cook gently for a further 30 minutes, stirring frequently until the rice is tender and has absorbed all the coconut milk. The mixture should be thick and creamy. Divide the rice pudding between 4 pudding bowls and top each portion with a tablespoonful of plain soya yogurt. Sprinkle with the coconut shreds to serve.

BAKED CHOCOLATE PUDDINGS WITH CHOCOLATE SAUCE

These individual puddings are wonderfully light due to the addition of egg whites. A delicious chocolate sauce is poured over the sponges to serve, soaking into them to create a rich and highly chocolatey dessert.

1   Preheat the oven to 190°C, gas mark 5. Grease 6 individual 175 ml pudding or oval dariole moulds with oil. Then use a little of the grated chocolate to coat the inside of each mould with a fine layer.

2   To prepare the chocolate puddings, melt the remaining grated chocolate in a heatproof bowl placed over a saucepan of simmering water. Beat the margarine and egg yolks with half the sugar in a separate bowl until thick and creamy, then stir in the melted chocolate.

3   Sift the flour and cocoa powder into the chocolate mixture and fold it in. Whisk the egg whites in a separate bowl until stiff. Gradually whisk the remaining sugar into the egg whites, then fold into the chocolate mixture. Divide the mixture between the prepared moulds and bake in the oven for 15 minutes until well risen and springy. Run a knife between the puddings and the moulds (if necessary) and turn them out on to warmed serving dishes. Pour over the Chocolate Sauce (see below) to serve.

Oil for greasing

175 g plain chocolate, finely grated

85 g non-dairy margarine

3 eggs, medium-sized, separated

175 g caster sugar

20 g plain flour

85 ml cocoa powder

500 ml Chocolate Sauce (see below)

Serves 6

CHOCOLATE SAUCE

Place 100 g of chopped plain chocolate and 400 ml of soya milk in a saucepan. Heat gently, stirring constantly until the chocolate melts. Mix 3 tablespoons of soya milk with 2 tablespoons each of cornflour and granulated sugar. Whisk into the chocolate milk in the pan. Bring to a boil, reduce the heat and simmer for 3 minutes, stirring constantly until the sauce thickens. (Makes 500 ml.)

BAKED MINI PINEAPPLES

Baby pineapples are filled with fresh fruit and topped with meringue before being baked briefly, resulting in a light and warm fruit dessert.

1   Preheat the oven to 220°C, gas mark 7. Slice the baby pineapples in half lengthways and remove the flesh using a knife, keeping the skins intact. Chop the flesh into cubes and mix with the mango and strawberries.

2   Arrange the pineapple shells side-by-side on a baking sheet, spoon the fruit into the shells and pour over the kirsch. Whisk the egg whites until stiff but not dry, then gradually whisk in the caster sugar until the mixture is stiff and glossy. Spoon or pipe this over the fruit to cover, then bake in the preheated oven for 5 minutes until the meringue is pale golden.

2 baby pineapples

1 large ripe mango, peeled and cubed

225 g strawberries

2 tablespoons kirsch

3 egg whites

175 g caster sugar

Serves 4

HOT FRUIT SOUFFLE WITH SLOE GIN-MACERATED FRUITS

FOR THE SOUFFLE

Oil for greasing

40 g sunflower margarine

40 g plain flour

170 g concentrated frozen orange juice, defrosted (170 ml once thawed)

50 g caster sugar

2 tablespoons fresh orange juice

4 egg whites

FOR THE FRUITS

450 g prepared mixed red berries, such as small strawberries, raspberries, cherries or redcurrants

4 tablespoons sloe or damson gin or cassis

Fresh mint sprigs to decorate

Serves 4

Sloe gin-soaked fruits are served topped with a light orange soufflé in this tasty pudding. If you are unable to find sloe or damson gin then use cassis which is readily available in supermarkets. This dessert can be made using either fresh or frozen fruits and enjoyed all year.

1   Preheat the oven to 200ºC, gas mark 6. Grease a 1.15 litre soufflé dish with oil and coat it with caster sugar, which helps the soufflé stick to the sides of the dish as it rises.

2   To prepare the soufflé, melt the sunflower margarine in a saucepan and stir in the flour. Remove the pan from the heat and gradually add the orange juice and 100 ml water. Bring to a boil, stirring constantly. Reduce the heat and simmer for 1 minute until a smooth, thick orange paste is formed. Remove the pan from the heat and stir in the sugar and fresh orange juice.

3   Whisk the egg whites in a bowl until stiff, then gradually whisk them into the orange mixture. Pour this mixture into the prepared soufflé dish and bake in the oven for 15–20 minutes until golden and firm to touch.

4   Meanwhile, place a mixture of strawberries, raspberries, cherries and redcurrants in a single layer on 4 individual serving plates and pour over the sloe or damson gin. Leave to macerate for 15–20 minutes while the soufflé is cooking.

5   Remove the soufflé from the oven, divide it into 4 portions and spoon on top of the macerated fruits. Place a sprig of mint on each helping to serve.

HOT COFFEE SOUFFLE

Oil for greasing

25 g non-dairy margarine

1 tablespoon plain flour

115 ml soya milk

115 ml hot strong black coffee

4 eggs, medium-sized, separated

50 g caster sugar

Icing sugar for dusting

Serves 4

This coffee soufflé uses ingredients found in most kitchen cupboards so is a marvellous standby for when entertaining unexpected guests.

1   Preheat the oven to 190ºC, gas mark 5. Grease a 1.15 litre soufflé dish with oil. Melt the margarine in a saucepan and stir in the flour. Remove from the heat and gradually stir in the soya milk, then the coffee. Place the pan back on the heat and bring the sauce to a boil, stirring constantly, then simmer for 2 minutes. Remove from the heat and leave to cool.

2   Beat the egg yolks and sugar until thick and fold into the cooled coffee sauce. Whisk the egg whites in a bowl until stiff and fold into the coffee mixture. Spoon this mixture into the soufflé dish and place in a roasting tin half filled with boiled water. Bake in the oven for 40 minutes until well risen and just firm to touch. Dust with icing sugar to serve.

SOUFFLE OMELETTE WITH CARAMELIZED ORCHARD FRUITS

This light and fluffy sweet soufflé omelette is very quick and easy to prepare and goes wonderfully well with a filling of autumn fruits.

1 To prepare the sauce, place the apples and pears in a large saucepan and add the apricot jam. Cook gently over low heat for 10 minutes until the fruits become soft. Stir in the Cointreau and set aside.

2 To prepare the soufflé, whisk the egg whites in a bowl until stiff but not dry. Beat the egg yolks with the vanilla sugar in a separate bowl until thick and creamy and fold into the whisked egg whites.

3 Preheat the grill to the highest setting. Heat a non-stick omelette pan or small frying pan over medium heat on the hob. Spoon the egg mixture into the pan and cook for 2 minutes until golden underneath. Place the pan under the preheated grill for 2–3 minutes until the top is golden and puffy.

4 Using a palette knife make a small indentation along the centre of the omelette, taking care not to cut all the way through. Spoon the fruit filling on to one half, fold the omelette over and carefully transfer to a serving plate. Sprinkle liberally with icing sugar and cut in half to serve.

FOR THE SAUCE

2 dessert apples, peeled, cored and sliced

2 pears, peeled, cored and sliced

2 tablespoons apricot jam

1 tablespoon Cointreau

FOR THE SOUFFLE OMELETTE

3 eggs, medium-sized, separated

2 tablespoons vanilla sugar (store caster sugar in a jar with a split vanilla pod)

Sifted icing sugar for sprinkling

Serves 2

BLUEBERRY CLAFOUTIS

Fresh blueberries baked with a dairy-free batter topping make a delicious change from the more traditional cherry clafoutis.

1 Preheat the oven to 220°C, gas mark 7. Arrange the blueberries in a 1.5 litre shallow oval dish.

2 Beat together the eggs, flour and caster sugar in a bowl until smooth. Place the soya milk in a saucepan and heat it gently. Gradually whisk it into the egg mixture. Pour the batter over the blueberries and dot with the margarine. Bake in the preheated oven for 30 minutes until the batter is puffed and golden on top. Serve hot.

350 g fresh blueberries

3 eggs, medium-sized

40 g plain flour

50 g caster sugar

430 ml soya milk

15 g non-dairy margarine

Serves 4

CREME BRULEE

This non-dairy version (see left) of the great French pudding (which is traditionally made with cream, eggs and sugar) is so delicious, you will keep coming back for more!

1 Mix together the orange rind and yogurt in a bowl. Then gently fold in the raspberries, taking care not to crush them.

2 Preheat the grill to the highest setting. Divide the raspberry and yogurt mixture between 6 individual 150 ml ramekins and carefully sprinkle the caster sugar evenly over the top of each portion.

3 Place the ramekins under the very hot grill for 4–5 minutes, until the sugar caramelizes to a crunchy topping with a rich golden brown colour. It is important to keep an eye on the ramekins to ensure the sugar browns evenly and does not burn.

4 Leave the Crème Brûlées to stand for a maximum of 30 minutes before serving – if they stand for any longer the caramel topping will soften.

Grated rind of 1 orange

500 g plain soya yogurt

225 g raspberries

200 g caster sugar

Serves 6

TOFFEE BANANAS

Bananas are partially cooked in a 'creamy' toffee sauce, then flamed with brandy to enhance the flavour. To impress your dinner guests, take the dessert to the table still flaming.

1 Place the brown sugar with 2 tablespoons of cold water in a shallow frying pan. Heat gently until the sugar dissolves.

2 Increase the heat and bring the mixture to a boil. Continue to cook for 3–5 minutes until the sugar begins to caramelize. Remove from the heat and pour the non-dairy cream into the pan. Return to the heat and whisk until the mixture thickens.

3 Arrange the bananas side-by-side in a single layer in the toffee mixture and return the pan to the heat. Cook gently for 8–10 minutes until heated through. Then, if desired, pour the brandy over the top and ignite it with a taper. Serve immediately.

125 g soft, light brown sugar

150 ml non-dairy cream

4 bananas, medium-sized, peeled and halved

2 tablespoons brandy (optional)

Serves 4

WARM SPICED FRUIT COMPOTE

500 g ready-to-eat dried fruits, such as figs, apricots, prunes or apple rings

1 cinnamon stick, halved

6 cloves

1 piece stem ginger, 3 cm, finely chopped

600 ml sweet cider

Grated rind and juice of 1 orange

1 tablespoon clear honey (or to taste)

Serves 6

Dried fruits are gently cooked in cider with cinnamon to create this warming winter dessert. You can make the pudding smarter by adding red wine in place of cider or make it suitable for children by using fresh orange juice instead of alcohol.

1 Place the dried fruit in a large saucepan and add the cinnamon stick, cloves and ginger. Toss gently, pour over the cider and mix well.

2 Slowly bring the fruit mixture to a boil over medium heat. Add the orange rind and juice and the honey. Reduce the heat and simmer for 10 minutes until the fruit is very tender. Remove the pan from the heat and spoon the fruits into serving bowls. Serve warm with Coconut Ice Cream (see page 109). Alternatively, chill in the refrigerator and serve cold with a dollop of plain soya yogurt.

POACHED PEARS

355 ml bottle dessert wine

175 g caster sugar

Thinly pared rind and juice of 1 lemon

1 cinnamon stick, halved

1 vanilla pod, split

6 green cardamom pods, lightly crushed

6 even-sized pears, such as William's, peeled

Serves 6

Whole pears, as they are poached, absorb the bold flavours of sweet wine, aromatic spices, lemon and vanilla in this refreshing dessert (see left) – a perfect end to any meal. I find the best sweet wine to use is Barsac which is better value than Sauternes.

1 Pour the dessert wine into a saucepan that is large enough for all the pears to lay flat. Add the caster sugar, the lemon rind and juice, the cinnamon stick, the vanilla pod and the green cardamoms. Heat gently until the sugar dissolves.

2 Slice the bases of the pears so that they stand upright. Place them in the pan on their sides and cook gently until the liquid just begins to simmer.

3 Cover the pan with a large sheet of greaseproof paper and simmer for 25 minutes. Turn the pears over carefully, re-cover with the greaseproof paper and simmer for a further 25 minutes until tender. Lift the pears from the pan using a slotted spoon and stand on a serving platter.

4 Boil the pear and wine liquid rapidly for 5 minutes, until syrupy and golden brown. Spoon the syrup over the pears and serve warm with plain soya yogurt.

FRESH FRUIT TERRINE

This fabulous dish consists of fresh fruits set in an orange juice jelly – ideal for summertime lunch parties.

1 Line a 1.7 litre terrine with clingfilm. Pour the orange juice into a saucepan and heat until the liquid is just about to boil. Remove the pan from the heat, then add the gelatine crystals. Stir constantly until the gelatine dissolves completely. Leave to cool for 15 minutes.

2 Prepare the fruits – halve or quarter any large strawberries, peel and chop the mangoes and peaches and halve the grapes. Mix the fruits together and arrange them attractively in the prepared terrine.

3 Pour the orange juice over the fruits and chill in the refrigerator for at least 3 hours until set. Turn out on to a chilled plate and peel away the clingfilm. Decorate the terrine with strawberries and fresh mint leaves.

600 ml orange juice

22 g gelatine crystals

900 g mixed summer fruits, such as strawberries, blueberries, mangoes, peaches, green grapes or raspberries

100 g strawberries to decorate

Sprigs of fresh mint leaves to decorate

Serves 6–8

UPSIDE-DOWN FRUIT TART

Forget the calories for a moment and tuck into this tasty apricot and sponge tart, which is delicious served warm with plain soya yogurt.

1 Preheat the oven to 180°C, gas mark 4. Lightly grease a 20.5 cm round cake tin with oil.

2 To prepare the filling, place the sugar in a heavy-based saucepan with 3 tablespoons of cold water. Heat gently until the sugar dissolves fully. Bring the mixture to a boil, then simmer gently for 3–5 minutes until it turns a golden colour. Pour this caramel over the base of the prepared cake tin and arrange the apricot halves over the top so they set in the caramel.

3 To prepare the sponge, sift the flour into a bowl and using your fingertips, rub in the margarine until the mixture resembles fine breadcrumbs. Stir in the beaten eggs and caster sugar using a wooden spoon. Spoon the mixture over the apricots and smooth out the surface.

4 Bake in the preheated oven for 30–35 minutes until the sponge is golden and springy to touch. Leave the cake to cool in the tin for 5 minutes, then turn it out on to a serving plate, so the fruit is on the top. Serve warm with plain soya yogurt.

FOR THE FILLING

Oil for greasing

175 g granulated sugar

900 g fresh apricots, halved and stoned

FOR THE SPONGE

175 g self-raising flour

100 g non-dairy margarine

2 eggs, medium-sized, beaten

25 g caster sugar

Plain soya yogurt to serve

Serves 6

UPSIDE-DOWN PLUM TART

Replace the apricots with 900 g of stoned and halved plums. To prepare the sponge, add half a teaspoon of mixed spice to the flour and replace the caster sugar with 25 g of soft, light brown sugar. Cook as instructed above.

INDIVIDUAL SUMMER PUDDINGS

900 g fresh summer fruits such as redcurrants, blackcurrants, strawberries, raspberries, cherries or blackberries, plus extra to serve

125 g granulated sugar

1 tablespoon cassis or blackcurrant cordial

12 slices white bread, medium-sliced, crusts removed

Mint leaves and white currants to serve

Serves 6

This classic English dessert of berries encased in juice-soaked moulded bread is here made in individual portions (see right). Summer puddings can be enjoyed all year round – simply prepare and freeze them in the summer months, when the fruit is fresh, then serve them in the winter to bring some sunshine to your table.

1   Place all the fruit in a large saucepan with the sugar and cassis or blackcurrant cordial. Heat gently for 5 minutes until the sugar dissolves and the fruit begins to soften. Remove from the heat and set aside.

2   Line 6 individual 150 ml moulds with 6 slices of bread, cut into quarters, reserving 6 slices, cut into small circles, to fill the base and to cover the moulds. Ensure the bread lines the moulds entirely, with no gaps left between slices (if using metal moulds, line them first with clingfilm).

3   Divide the fruit mixture into 6 portions and spoon it into the bread-lined moulds. Top each pudding with the reserved bread, then cover with clingfilm. Sit a saucer over each mould and weight it down – this pressure helps to pack the fruit into the mould and allows the juices to seep into the bread. Leave the puddings in the refrigerator to stand overnight.

4   Remove the weights and clingfilm and turn the moulds out on to serving plates. Garnish with mint leaves and white currants to serve.

ORCHARD STRUDEL

300 g Victoria plums, stoned and chopped

300 g eating apples, peeled, cored and chopped

300 g pears, peeled, cored and chopped

150 g granulated sugar

160 g filo pastry, 10 sheets measuring approximately 40 x 30 cm

2 teaspoons ground nutmeg

300 ml non-dairy cream, 3 tablespoons Calvados or orange juice and white currants to serve (optional)

Serves 6

Fresh plums, apples and pears are ideal for cooking in thin sheets of filo pastry. However, a mixture of dried fruits soaked in a little orange juice can be used as an alternative if fresh fruits are not available.

1   Preheat the oven to 190°C, gas mark 5. Place the fruit in a saucepan with the sugar and cook gently for 5 minutes until the sugar dissolves and the fruit softens.

2   Lay a sheet of filo pastry on a work surface and sprinkle with a little of the ground nutmeg. Top with another sheet of filo and repeat until all but 2 of the filo sheets have been used. Cover the remaining 2 sheets with a damp tea towel to prevent them from drying out.

3   Spoon the fruit along one edge of the pastry. Tuck in the ends and roll up the strudel loosely. Cut the reserved filo pastry into strips, scrunch them into rosettes and arrange them on top of the strudel. Place the strudel on a large baking sheet and bake in the preheated oven for 20 minutes until the pastry is golden. Serve sliced, with non-dairy cream flavoured with Calvados or orange juice, if desired, and garnish with white currants.

RASPBERRY ICE MERINGUE NEST

This impressive meringue nest filled with raspberry ice (see left) is a good dessert for making ahead of time – the meringue stays fresh in an airtight container for up to two weeks and the raspberry ice can be frozen for up to three months. The same amount of fresh blueberries or strawberries can be used instead of the raspberries as an alternative.

1 Preheat the oven to 110°C, gas mark ¼. Line a baking sheet with baking parchment. In the centre of the parchment draw a 23 cm circle using a pencil, then turn the paper over so that you can still clearly see the circle through the paper.

2 To prepare the meringue, whisk the egg whites until stiff but not dry and greatly increased in volume. Whisk in half the caster sugar until the mixture is stiff and glossy. Then whisk in the remaining sugar, adding the vanilla essence with the last of the sugar.

3 Spread a layer of meringue on the baking parchment to fill the marked circle. Then spoon the remaining meringue mixture into a piping bag fitted with a large star nozzle and carefully pipe a rim around the edge of the meringue circle. If you do not have a piping bag, mould the meringue into ovals using 2 dessert spoons and sit the ovals around the edge of the meringue circle to form a wall. Bake the nest in the preheated oven for 2 hours until crisp and dry. Turn off the heat and leave the meringue to cool in the oven, then peel off the baking parchment.

4 To make the raspberry ice, heat the soya milk with the cinnamon stick in a large saucepan over low heat until the milk begins to steam, then remove from the heat and set aside.

5 Whisk the egg yolks, sugar and cornflour in a large mixing bowl until pale, then gradually add the heated milk. Place the mixture in a saucepan and cook gently for 5 minutes, stirring constantly until slightly thickened. Remove from the heat and leave to cool. Strain the cooled custard through a sieve and place in a bowl. Stir in the soya yogurt.

6 Place the raspberries in a food processor and blend until puréed, then sieve the mixture, if wished – this removes all the pips, producing a smoother purée. (Alternatively, if you do not have a food processor, pass the fresh raspberries through a sieve.)

7 Stir the raspberry purée into the custard mixture and pour into a rigid container. Freeze for 3 hours until the mixture begins to set. Remove the mixture from the freezer and beat until smooth. Then return to the freezer for 4–5 hours until the mixture is solid.

8 When ready to serve, place the meringue on a serving plate and fill with scoops of the raspberry ice. Decorate with fresh redcurrants, if desired.

FOR THE MERINGUE

3 egg whites

175 g caster sugar

1 teaspoon vanilla essence

FOR THE RASPBERRY ICE

300 ml soya milk

1 cinnamon stick, broken

3 egg yolks

125 g caster sugar

1 tablespoon cornflour

300 ml plain soya yogurt

250 g fresh raspberries

Fresh redcurrants to decorate (optional)

Serves 8

Mango Sorbet

410 g canned mango slices

300 ml pure tropical fruit juice

3 egg whites

Serves 8

Sorbets are made from a basic mixture of sugar, water and egg whites flavoured with fruit. I have used mango slices and tropical fruit drink in this refreshing low-fat dessert. If you are uncomfortable using raw eggs, simply omit the egg white and serve this as a granita (see below).

1 Drain the mango slices, place them in a food processor and blend until smooth. With the motor running, gradually add the tropical fruit juice and 150 ml cold water. (Alternatively, pass the mango slices through a sieve and whisk in the fruit drink and water.) Sieve into a freezerproof container then freeze for 2–3 hours until thick, slushy and almost set.

2 Place the partially frozen mango mixture in a food processor and blend until smooth or beat the mixture by hand.

3 Whisk the egg whites until stiff. Fold into the mango mixture then return to the freezer for 4–5 hours until solid. Scoop into bowls to serve.

MELON SORBET

For a delicious melon sorbet, use 1 kg of either Cantaloupe or Honeydew melon. Remove the flesh and blend it in a food processor with the juice of 2 lemons and 250 g of icing sugar. Once the mixture is smooth, pour it into a shallow container and freeze until slushy. Process again, then return the mixture to the freezer for 4–5 hours until solid.

Strawberry Granita

250 g fresh strawberries

1 tablespoon icing sugar

300 ml sweet white wine

Serves 4

Granita, a popular Italian dessert, is simply frozen flavoured liquid that is scraped with a fork to create its characteristic granular texture.

1 Place the strawberries in a food processor and blend until smooth. Sieve the purée to remove the pips. Stir in the icing sugar and sweet wine, place the mixture in a shallow tray and freeze for 4 hours until solid.

2 Scrape the frozen mixture with a fork to produce crystals, then spoon it into chilled glasses to serve.

TROPICAL GRANITA

Cut 6 passion fruits in half and scoop out the seeds using a spoon. Mix these with 150 ml each of orange juice and fresh mango juice. Strain, then freeze and scrape as described above.

COCONUT ICE CREAM WITH CURRIED FRUIT SALAD

This dairy-free ice cream is served with a warm, exotic mixture of spiced fruits. For extra flavour, puréed red fruits such as strawberries or raspberries, or the grated rind and juice of a lime can be added to the basic ice cream mixture.

1 To prepare the ice cream, place the coconut milk in a large saucepan and heat gently until it begins to bubble. Remove from the heat. Whisk together the eggs and sugar in a mixing bowl until pale. Continue to whisk while adding the heated coconut milk in a steady stream.

2 Leave the mixture to cool, stirring occasionally. Pour into a freezerproof container and freeze for 3 hours. Remove from the freezer and scoop the ice cream into a food processor. Process until smooth. Pour back into the freezerproof container and return to the freezer for 4–5 hours until solid.

3 To make the fruit salad, place the orange rind and juice in a saucepan with the coriander seeds, turmeric, cumin and sugar. Heat gently for 5 minutes until the sugar dissolves.

4 Add the prepared fruits to the pan and heat gently for 5 minutes until the fruits are soft and just cooked. Leave to cool. Divide the fruit mixture between 6 dessert bowls and top with a scoop of ice cream to serve.

FOR THE ICE CREAM

800 ml coconut milk

4 medium-sized eggs

85 g caster sugar

FOR THE CURRIED FRUIT SALAD

Grated rind and juice of 1 large orange

2 teaspoons coriander seeds

1 teaspoon ground turmeric

1 teaspoon ground cumin

2 tablespoons caster sugar

2 mangoes, peeled, stoned and sliced

1 pineapple, peeled, cored and sliced

150 g physalis, paper-like husk removed

Serves 6

7

Cakes & Breads

CHESTNUT LOG

Chestnuts are in season between September and February – perfect for Christmas time, as is this rich chestnut sponge filled with a chocolate 'cream'. Decorate this cake with marrons glacé (chestnuts preserved in sweet syrup), if desired.

FOR THE SPONGE

Oil for greasing

4 eggs, medium-sized

150 g caster sugar

Few drops of vanilla extract

50 g cooked chestnuts, mashed

100 g plain flour

1 tablespoon icing sugar

FOR THE FILLING

85 g plain chocolate, melted

175 ml plain soya yogurt

Icing sugar and cocoa powder, sifted for dusting (optional)

Serves 8

1 Preheat the oven to 200°C, gas mark 6. Grease a 30 x 20 x 3 cm Swiss roll tin with oil and line it with greaseproof paper.

2 To prepare the cake, whisk the eggs, sugar and vanilla extract in a bowl until they are thick and creamy and a ribbon-like trail forms when the whisks are lifted from the mixture. Fold in the mashed chestnuts and flour.

3 Spoon the mixture into the prepared tin and bake in the preheated oven for 15 minutes until risen and springy to touch.

4 Lay a sheet of greaseproof paper on a work surface and sift the icing sugar over it. Remove the cake from the oven and carefully turn it out on to the greaseproof paper. Leave to cool.

5 To prepare the filling, break the chocolate into a bowl and place over a saucepan of simmering water until melted. Remove from the heat, add the yogurt and beat until smooth. Spread the sponge with the chocolate mixture. Trim the edges of the sponge to neaten and, using the sheet of greaseproof paper, roll the cake along the short edge to form a 'log'. Dust with sifted icing sugar and cocoa powder to serve.

SPICY SYRUP CAKE

This moist maple syrup cake gets its spicy taste from chopped ginger. Lemon icing makes a fitting topping.

Oil for greasing

175 g non-dairy margarine

175 g soft, light brown sugar

3 eggs, medium-sized

3 tablespoons maple syrup

2 bulbs stem ginger, each bulb weighing approximately 15 g, chopped

350 g self-raising flour

100 g granulated sugar

Juice of 1 small lemon

Serves 8

1 Preheat the oven to 180°C, gas mark 4. Lightly grease a 20.5 cm square cake tin with oil and line it with greaseproof paper.

2 Beat the margarine and the brown sugar in a mixing bowl until pale and fluffy. Then gradually beat in the eggs and maple syrup. Fold in the chopped ginger and the sifted flour. Spoon the mixture into the prepared tin and bake in the preheated oven for 1 hour.

3 Meanwhile place the sugar and lemon juice in a small saucepan. Cook gently over low heat until the sugar completely dissolves. Increase the heat and boil for 2 minutes. Remove the cake from the oven, turn out on to a plate and drizzle over the lemon syrup while the cake is still warm.

CARROT CAKE

The mashed bananas give this carrot cake (see above) its moist texture and delicious flavour. Keep it for four days in an airtight container or for one month in the freezer.

1 Preheat the oven to 180°C, gas mark 4. Grease a 20.5 cm round cake tin with oil and line it with greaseproof paper.

2 Sift the flour and baking powder into a large bowl and mix in the brown sugar. Stir in the mashed bananas, grated carrots, beaten eggs and oil and beat until the mixture is runny. Pour the mixture into the prepared tin and bake in the preheated oven for 45–60 minutes. The cake is cooked when it shrinks from the edges of the tin, is firm to touch and golden in colour.

3 Leave the cake to cool a little in the tin for 10 minutes before turning it out on to a wire rack to cool completely. Remove the lining paper and serve the cake cut into slices.

Oil for greasing

300 g self-raising flour

1 teaspoon baking powder

175 g soft, light brown sugar

2 bananas, medium-sized, mashed

175 g carrots, scrubbed and grated

3 eggs, medium-sized, beaten

180 ml sunflower oil

Serves 8

CHOCOLATE CAKE BARS

These Chocolate Cake Bars (see left) are deliciously gooey because they are made with oil rather than butter. It is best to leave them wrapped up for a day or two before serving as they become increasingly moist and tasty as they keep.

1　Preheat the oven to 180°C, gas mark 4. Grease a 20.5 cm square cake tin with oil and line the base with greaseproof paper.

2　Sift the flour with the baking powder into a large mixing bowl and stir in the brown sugar. Beat the cocoa and water mixture with the oil and the eggs in a separate bowl. Then beat this into the flour mixture until smooth. Finally, stir in the chopped chocolate.

3　Spoon the cake mixture into the prepared tin and bake in the preheated oven for 45–50 minutes until risen and cooked through. To test if the cake is cooked, insert a skewer into the middle of the cake – if it comes out clean the cake is cooked through. Turn out on to a wire rack to cool, then cut into bars to serve.

Oil for greasing

300 g self-raising flour

1 teaspoon baking powder

175 g soft, light brown sugar

2 tablespoons cocoa powder, dissolved in an equal amount of boiling water

175 ml sunflower oil

3 eggs, medium-sized, beaten

50 g plain chocolate, chopped

Makes 16 bars

MOCHA BARS

To brighten up any mid-morning coffee break, serve these chocolate and coffee flavoured bars. They can be frozen un-iced for up to two months.

1　Preheat the oven to 190°C, gas mark 5. Grease a 17.5 cm square cake tin with oil and line it with greaseproof paper.

2　To prepare the cake, beat the eggs and sugar in a bowl until they are thick and creamy and a ribbon-like trail forms when the whisks are lifted from the mixture. Fold in the grated chocolate, sifted flour, then the coffee. Spoon the mixture into the prepared tin.

3　Bake in the preheated oven for 20 minutes until well risen and springy to touch. Leave the cake in the tin for 5 minutes before turning out on to a wire rack to cool.

4　To make the icing, mix the icing sugar with the coffee and sufficient warm water to make a smooth icing. Melt the chocolate in a bowl placed over a saucepan of simmering water. Spoon the melted chocolate into a piping bag fitted with a small plain 'nozzle'.

5　Spread the coffee icing over the top of the cake. Decorate it by piping lines of chocolate horizontally across the icing, roughly 2 cm apart. Using a skewer or cocktail stick, draw lines vertically through the chocolate in both directions to give a feather-like effect. Cut the cake into bars to serve.

FOR THE CAKE

Oil for greasing

4 eggs, medium-sized

125 g golden caster sugar

50 g plain chocolate, finely grated

125 g plain flour, sifted

3 tablespoons strong, black filter coffee

FOR THE ICING

150 g icing sugar, sifted

1 tablespoon strong, black filter coffee

25 g plain chocolate, chopped

Makes 14 bars

SIMPLE FRUIT CAKE

Oil for greasing

680 g dried mixed fruit, such as raisins, sultanas, mixed peel, chopped apricots or chopped prunes

300 ml fresh apple juice

175 g non-dairy margarine

175 g soft, light brown sugar

3 eggs, medium-sized, beaten

200 g self-raising flour

Serves 8

Fruit cake is so often served just at Christmas or Easter, which is a great shame in my opinion. This delicious cake is perfect for serving at any time of the year.

1   Preheat the oven to 150°C, gas mark 2. Grease a 20.5 cm round cake tin with oil and line it with greaseproof paper.

2   Place the mixed fruits in a large saucepan, pour over the apple juice and bring the mixture to a boil. Reduce the heat and simmer for 20 minutes. Remove the pan from the heat and leave to cool.

3   Cream the margarine and brown sugar in a large mixing bowl until pale. Gradually beat in the eggs, then fold in the flour and mixed fruit. Spoon the mixture into the prepared cake tin and bake in the oven for 3¼–3½ hours. Remove from the oven and leave in the tin for 5 minutes, then turn out on to a wire rack to cool.

STRAWBERRY & CARDAMOM ROLL

FOR THE SPONGE

Oil for greasing

3 tablespoons green cardamom pods

85 g plain flour

3 eggs, medium-sized

85 g caster sugar

FOR THE FILLING

Icing sugar for dusting

150 ml strawberry-flavoured soya yogurt

100 g strawberries, hulled and chopped

Serves 6

Adding cardamom to this Swiss roll mixture produces a cake with a fascinating flavour which is complemented perfectly by strawberry soya yogurt and fresh strawberries.

1   Preheat the oven to 200°C, gas mark 6. Grease a 20.5 x 30.5 x 2 cm Swiss roll tin with oil and line it with greaseproof paper.

2   Remove the cardamom seeds from the pods and crush them coarsely in a mortar with a pestle. Sift the flour into a bowl and set aside.

3   Whisk the eggs and the sugar in a separate bowl until they are thick and creamy and a ribbon-like trail forms when the whisks are lifted from the mixture. Fold in the flour and cardamom seeds, then pour the mixture into the prepared tin and bake in the oven for 12–15 minutes.

4   Dust a large sheet of greaseproof paper with icing sugar, then turn the cooked sponge out on to it. Trim the edges to neaten and roll from a short edge, leaving the greaseproof paper in the roll. Set aside and leave to cool. When cool, unroll and spread the yogurt over the sponge, scatter the strawberries over the top and reroll the sponge without the greaseproof paper. Dust with icing sugar to serve.

FRESH FRUIT TARTLETS

These individual pastry cases, made with filo pastry, can be filled with a variety of delicious ingredients – here I have used plain soya yogurt flavoured with orange rind and honey and topped with fresh summer fruits (see right). Fruit tartlets never fail to impress your guests and are ideal to serve at a summer tea party.

1 Preheat the oven to 190°C, gas mark 5. To make the cases, cut the filo pastry into 32 squares. Gently press a square of the pastry into a 4 cm tartlet tin and sprinkle lightly with cinnamon. Lay a second square of pastry on top of the first, at an angle (so the pastry edge is ragged) and press gently into the tin. Set aside and repeat with the other tartlet tins until all the filo pastry is used up – you should have 16 pastry cases.

2 Bake the cases in the preheated oven for 5 minutes until the pastry is pale golden in colour. Remove from the oven and leave to cool, then carefully remove the pastry cases from the tartlet tins and set aside.

3 To make the filling, beat the yogurt with the orange rind and honey in a bowl until well blended. Carefully spoon this mixture into the cooled pastry cases and arrange the summer fruits on top.

4 Place the redcurrant jelly in a small saucepan. Cook over low heat until it melts and becomes runny. Then gently brush the melted jelly over the fruits to glaze. Serve the tartlets cold.

65 g filo pastry, 4 sheets measuring approximately 40 cm x 30 cm

2–3 teaspoons ground cinnamon for sprinkling

170 ml plain soya yogurt

Finely grated rind of 1 orange

2 teaspoons clear honey

500 g summer fruits, such as raspberries, strawberries or blueberries

125 g redcurrant jelly

Makes 16

MARZIPAN BAKLAVA

This lactose-free recipe is an adaptation of the Middle Eastern Baklava, a sweet dessert traditionally made of many layers of butter-drenched filo pastry, spices and chopped nuts. Unsurprisingly, it has been a popular dessert since the heyday of the Ottoman Empire.

1 Preheat the oven to 180°C, gas mark 4. Lightly grease a 25 x 20 cm baking dish with oil. Place a sheet of filo pastry over the base of the baking dish and top with a little of the apple purée and chopped marzipan. Continue to layer the pastry, purée and marzipan in this way, finishing with a layer of pastry. Score the top layer into squares or triangles and bake in the preheated oven for 45 minutes until golden.

2 A couple of minutes before removing the cooked Baklava from the oven, heat the honey in a saucepan with the cinnamon over low heat until runny. Remove the Baklava from the oven, drizzle the honey over the top and leave to stand for 5 minutes. Cut into triangles or squares to serve.

Oil for greasing

375 g filo pastry, 24 sheets measuring approximately 40 cm x 30 cm

450 g apple purée

325 g marzipan, chopped

125 ml clear honey

1 teaspoon ground cinnamon

Makes 15 pieces

CINNAMON SWIRL TEA RING

680 g strong plain flour

1 tablespoon salt

1 tablespoon ground cinnamon

25 g non-dairy margarine

11 g dried easy-blend yeast

Oil for greasing

100 g raisins

50 g soft, light brown sugar

Makes 800 g loaf

Raisins are rolled into cinnamon dough to make a pleasing spiral pattern, which is revealed once the cooked loaf is sliced (see above).

1 Sift the flour, salt and cinnamon into a bowl. Rub in the margarine and stir in the yeast. Add 430 ml lukewarm water and mix to make a soft, not sticky dough. Turn out on to a floured work surface and knead well for 10 minutes. Place the dough into an oiled bowl, then cover with greased clingfilm and leave in a warm place for 90 minutes until doubled in size.

2 Preheat the oven to 220°C, gas mark 7. Grease a 900 g loaf tin with oil. Knock back the dough and roll into a rectangle the same length as the tin but 3 times the width. Sprinkle over the raisins and roll up the dough from an edge that is the same length as the tin. Place into the tin and cover with oiled clingfilm. Leave in a warm place for 30 minutes. Bake in the oven for 10 minutes, then reduce the temperature to 190°C, gas mark 5 and bake for a further 25–30 minutes. Turn out on to a wire rack and leave to cool.

CITRUS RINGS WITH SUMMER BERRIES

A mixture of cherries, blackberries, raspberries and physalis is my choice of filling for these tasty citrus rings, but you can mix and match your own favourite summer fruit.

1 Grease 6 small 300 ml ring moulds (or savarin moulds) with oil. To prepare the citrus rings, stir together the flour, salt, yeast and sugar in a mixing bowl until well blended. Gradually work in the eggs and 300 ml hand-hot water. Then knead the dough on a floured work surface for 10 minutes.

2 Divide the dough into 6 portions, knead each one and shape into spheres. Using a floured finger, make a hole in the centre of each sphere and place it in a greased ring mould. Cover the filled moulds with greased clingfilm and leave them in a warm place for 45 minutes until the dough doubles in size. Preheat the oven to 220°C, gas mark 7.

3 Bake the bread rings in the preheated oven for 20 minutes until well risen and golden. Leave to cool in the tins for 5 minutes, then turn out on to a wire rack to cool completely.

4 Sift the icing sugar into a bowl and gradually add the lemon juice. Beat the mixture until smooth, drizzle over the bread rings, then transfer them to serving plates. To make the filling, spoon the soya yogurt into the centre of each bread ring. Divide the fruit into 6 portions and arrange a little of each portion on top of the yogurt and the remainder on the serving plate around the ring. Decorate each portion with fresh mint or fruit leaves and sift a generous sprinkling of icing sugar over each ring to serve.

FOR THE CITRUS RINGS

Oil for greasing

680 g strong plain flour

1 tablespoon salt

11 g dried easy-blend yeast

2 tablespoons caster sugar

2 eggs, medium-sized

175 g icing sugar

Juice of ½ lemon

FOR THE FILLING

150 ml plain soya yogurt

450 g summer fruit, such as cherries, blackberries, raspberries or physalis

Fresh mint or fruit leaves to decorate

Icing sugar for dusting

Serves 6

PEANUT BUTTER COOKIES

I could not believe my luck when I discovered that peanut butter is fantastic for making biscuits in place of butter. These cookies keep fresh in an airtight container for four days or can be frozen for one month.

1 Preheat the oven to 190°C, gas mark 5. Lightly grease 2 large baking sheets with oil. Beat together the peanut butter and yogurt in a mixing bowl. Add the caster sugar and mix well until all the ingredients are well blended. Beat in the egg and gradually add the flour until the mixture is smooth.

2 Cover the cookie mixture and chill in the refrigerator for 15 minutes. Then shape the mixture into 25 walnut-sized balls using your hands and place on the baking sheets, leaving plenty of room between each cookie. Flatten each of these with a fork to a thickness of 1 cm. Bake in the preheated oven for 10–12 minutes, then leave to cool on a wire rack before serving.

Oil for greasing

175 g crunchy peanut butter

2 tablespoons plain soya yogurt

150 g golden caster sugar

1 egg, medium-sized

150 g self-raising flour

Makes 25

SAVOURY TOMATO SCONES

Oil for greasing

300 g self-raising flour

1 tablespoon sun-dried tomato paste

120 ml plain soya yogurt, plus extra
to serve

2 eggs, medium-sized, beaten

Black and green olives, halved, 1 red and
1 yellow pepper, peeled and sliced thinly
to serve

Makes 12

*These savoury scones are ideal for picnics – use them instead of bread
with a selection of toppings, or simply eat them on their own.*

1 Preheat the oven to 220°C, gas mark 7. Lightly grease a large baking sheet
with a little oil.

2 Sift the flour into a mixing bowl. Beat together the sun-dried tomato paste,
soya yogurt and eggs in a separate bowl until smooth. Pour this mixture
into the flour and work to a soft, not sticky dough. Knead the dough on a
floured surface, then roll it out to a thickness of 2 cm. Use a plain, circular
pastry cutter to cut scone shapes – reroll the trimmings as necessary.

3 Arrange the scones on the prepared baking sheet and bake in the oven for
12–15 minutes until golden and well risen. Serve warm, split and topped
with soya yogurt, black and green olives and red and yellow peppers.

OLIVE SCONES

Omit the sun-dried tomato paste and, instead, stir 25 g of pitted and chopped
black or green olives into the flour. Stir in the yogurt and eggs as indicated
above. Roll out the dough on a lightly floured work surface into a circular
shape. Transfer to a baking sheet and mark into eight segments with the back
of a knife. Bake in the preheated oven for 15–20 minutes until risen and golden.
Serve the segments broken, with soups or cold meats and fish.

APRICOT SCONES

Oil for greasing

200 g self-raising flour

50 g caster sugar

85 g dried apricots, chopped

120 ml plain soya yogurt, plus extra
to serve

2 eggs, medium-sized, beaten

Strawberry or raspberry jam to serve

12 fresh strawberries to decorate

Makes 12

*Traditionally, sultanas or raisins are used to make sweet scones, but I
love the flavour of scones with dried apricots (dried mango is also
delicious). Top these scones with strawberry jam, plain soya yogurt
and fresh fruit for a tempting 'cream' tea (see right).*

1 Preheat the oven to 220°C, gas mark 7. Lightly grease a large baking sheet
with a little oil.

2 Sift the flour and sugar into a mixing bowl and stir in the apricots. Beat
together the yogurt and eggs in a separate bowl until smooth. Pour this
mixture into the flour and work to a soft, not sticky dough. Lightly knead
the dough on a floured surface. Roll out the dough to a thickness of 2 cm
and use a plain or fluted circular pastry cutter to make scones – reroll the
trimmings as necessary.

3 Arrange the scones on the baking sheet and bake in the preheated oven for
12–15 minutes until golden and well risen. Split and serve warm with fruit
jam and plain soya yogurt, topped with a fresh strawberry.

FOCACCIA

450 g strong plain flour

1 teaspoon salt

11 g dried easy-blend yeast

5 tablespoons extra virgin olive oil, plus extra for greasing

2 tablespoons chopped fresh thyme

2 teaspoons coarse sea salt

Fresh thyme sprigs to serve

Makes 450 g loaf

This Italian bread (see below – on table) is made from pizza dough and is baked in squares, then drizzled with olive oil and herbs.

1   Mix the flour, salt and yeast in a bowl. Add 3 tablespoons of the olive oil and 300 ml of tepid water. Stir to make a soft, not sticky dough. Knead for 5 minutes on a lightly floured surface. Transfer to an oiled bowl, cover with clingfilm and leave in a warm place for 45 minutes until doubled in size.

2   Preheat the oven to 200°C, gas mark 6. Lightly grease a baking sheet with olive oil. Turn out the dough on to a lightly floured surface and knead in the thyme. Shape the dough into a large oval and place on the prepared baking sheet. Using lightly floured fingers, press the dough to make random dents in the surface. Cover with greased clingfilm and leave in a warm place for 30 minutes until doubled in size.

3   Remove the clingfilm and bake the dough in the oven for 25 minutes until golden and risen. Drizzle the remaining 2 tablespoons of olive oil over the baked bread and scatter salt and thyme sprigs on top, then serve warm.

HERB BREAD ROLLS

Bought bread often contains dairy products, so it is better to make your own. These bread rolls (see opposite – in basket) contain fresh herbs.

1   Sift the flour and salt into a bowl. Stir in the yeast, then 450 ml tepid water. Using first a palette knife, then your hands, blend the mixture well. Turn out the dough on to a lightly floured surface, knead for 5 minutes until smooth and elastic, then place in an oiled bowl. Cover with greased clingfilm and leave in a warm place for 45 minutes until doubled in size.

2   Preheat the oven to 200°C, gas mark 6. Grease a baking sheet with oil. Turn out the dough on to a lightly floured surface, knead in the herbs, then shape into 12 even-sized ovals. Arrange them on the baking sheet. Cover with greased clingfilm and leave for 30 minutes in a warm place until doubled in size. Sprinkle with flour and bake in the preheated oven for 20 minutes until the rolls sound hollow when tapped on the bases.

450 g strong plain flour, plus extra for sprinkling

1 teaspoon salt

11 g dried easy-blend yeast

Oil for greasing

2 tablespoons chopped fresh sage, parsley or thyme

Makes 12

POPPY SEED ROLLS

Omit the chopped herbs. Divide the dough into 14 portions and shape these into spheres. Arrange in 2 oiled 17.5 cm sandwich tins. Cover with greased clingfilm and leave for 30 minutes in a warm place until the rolls are doubled in size and fill the tins. Sprinkle the rolls with poppy seeds and bake as above.

MALT LOAF

Fruity malt loaf is great at tea time – serve it warm or toast it and spread it with apricot conserve.

1   Mix the flours, yeast, salt, sugar and raisins in a bowl. Make a well in the centre and pour in the margarine, malt extract and treacle. Stir well then, using your hands, knead the dough for 5 minutes until soft and sticky. Turn into a bowl and cover with greased clingfilm. Leave in a warm place for 90 minutes until doubled in size.

2   Brush a 500 g loaf tin with oil. Knead the dough on a floured work surface until smooth. Place in the tin, cover with greased clingfilm and leave in a warm place for 45 minutes. Preheat the oven to 190°C, gas mark 5.

3   Bake the loaf in the oven for 45–50 minutes until well risen and cooked through. You may need to cover the loaf with greaseproof paper during cooking to prevent the top from burning.

4   Heat the sugar and the water in a small saucepan over low heat until the sugar dissolves. Increase the heat and simmer for 2 minutes. Remove the loaf from the oven, immediately brush with the glaze and serve warm.

225 g wholemeal flour

125 g strong plain flour

11 g dried easy-blend yeast

Pinch each of salt and sugar

85 g raisins

25 g non-dairy margarine, melted

2 tablespoons malt extract

2 teaspoons black treacle

Oil for greasing

2 tablespoons caster sugar

2 tablespoons water

Makes 500 g loaf

The nutritional information for each recipe refers to a single serving, unless otherwise stated. Optional ingredients are not included. The figures are intended as a guide only. If salt is given in a measured amount in the recipe it has been included in the analysis; if the recipe suggests adding a pinch of salt or seasoning to taste, salt has not been included.

p.10 French Onion Soup with Sun-dried Tomato Topping
233Kcals; 6g protein; 7g total fat; 1g saturated fat; 39g carbohydrate; 3g fibre; 357mg sodium; 96g calcium

p.10 Mixed Bean Soup
170–113Kcals; 8.5–6g protein; 6.5–4.5g total fat; 0.9–0.6g saturated fat; 20–13.5g carbohydrate; 8.6–6g fibre; 588–392mg sodium; 105–70mg calcium

p.11 Butternut Squash Soup
344Kcals; 6g protein; 17.5g total fat; 2.5g saturated fat; 44g carbohydrate; 5g fibre; 206mg sodium; 156mg calcium

p.12 Salmon & Saffron Risotto
373Kcals; 17g protein; 11g total fat; 2g saturated fat; 51g carbohydrate; 0.1g fibre; 28mg sodium; 27mg calcium

p.13 Lemon Thai Prawns
163Kcals; 6g protein; 15g total fat; 2g saturated fat; 1g carbohydrate; 0.1g fibre; 1163mg sodium; 32mg calcium

p.13 Golden Scallops with Spinach
107Kcals; 14g protein; 4.5g total fat; 1g saturated fat; 2.5g carbohydrate; 0.5g fibre; 136mg sodium; 53mg calcium

p.14 Chicken Satay
458 Kcals; 40g protein; 31g total fat; 18g saturated fat; 5g carbohydrate; 1g fibre; 192mg sodium; 23mg calcium

p.14 Pheasant in Parma Ham
306Kcals; 33g protein; 17g total fat; 4g saturated fat; 5g carbohydrate; 1g fibre; 298mg sodium; 74mg calcium

p.16 Toasted Ciabatta Sandwiches
725Kcals; 37g protein; 26g total fat; 4g saturated fat; 78g carbohydrate; 4.5g fibre; 1258mg sodium; 23mg calcium

p.16 Mini Pancakes with Bresaola & Arugula
219–146Kcals; 13–9g protein; 3.5–2.5g total fat; 0.7–0.5g saturated fat; 33–22g carbohydrate; 2–1g fibre; 851–567mg sodium; 133–88mg calcium

p.16 Roasted Vegetable Tarts
313Kcals; 7.5g protein; 16g total fat; 3g saturated fat; 36g carbohydrate; 4g fibre; 147mg sodium; 141mg calcium

p.18 Golden Asparagus with Lemon Pasta
237Kcals; 1.5g protein; 9.0g total fat; 1.5g saturated fat; 31.0g carbohydrate; 2g fibre; 7mg sodium; 16mg calcium

p.18 Mixed Bean Salad
96Kcals; 2g protein; 7.5g total fat; 1g saturated fat; 5.5g carbohydrate; 2g fibre; 114mg sodium; 21mg calcium

p.18 Grilled Chicory
241Kcals; 5g protein; 23g total fat; 2g saturated fat; 5g carbohydrate; 2g fibre; 2mg sodium; 41mg calcium

p.19 Caesar Salad
450Kcals; 12g protein; 37g total fat; 5g saturated fat; 18g carbohydrate; 1g fibre; 791mg sodium; 151mg calcium

p.22 Warm Mackerel & Potato Salad
500Kcals; 20g protein; 43g total fat; 8g saturated fat; 8.5g carbohydrate; 1g fibre; 768mg sodium; 40mg calcium

p.22 Pan-fried Mackerel with Orange and Rosemary
540Kcals; 39g protein; 41g total fat; 8g saturated fat; 5g carbohydrate; 1g fibre; 263mg sodium; 76mg calcium

p.24 Smoked Cod with Bacon
477Kcals; 50g protein; 16g total fat; 3g saturated fat; 36g carbohydrate; 2.5g fibre; 2268mg sodium; 75mg calcium

p.24 Plaice with Peppers
290Kcals; 29g protein; 15g total fat; 2g saturated fat; 10g carbohydrate; 3.5g fibre; 192mg sodium; 97mg calcium

p.25 Crispy Hake & Chips
863Kcals; 28.5g protein; 55g total fat; 12g saturated fat; 66g carbohydrate; 2.4g fibre; 610mg sodium; 45mg calcium

p.25 Potato-topped Fish Pie
722Kcals; 55g protein; 15.5g total fat; 3g saturated fat; 92g carbohydrate; 6g fibre; 1293mg sodium; 306mg calcium

p.27 Classic Kedgeree
391Kcals; 34g protein; 8g total fat; 2g saturated fat; 45g carbohydrate; 0g fibre; 940mg sodium; 70mg calcium

p.27 Salad Niçoise
616Kcals; 50g protein; 36g total fat; 6g saturated fat; 25g carbohydrate; 5g fibre; 1180mg sodium; 113mg calcium

p.28 Herb-coated Turkey
452Kcals; 28g protein; 4g total fat; 1g saturated fat; 80g carbohydrate; 1g fibre; 514mg sodium; 90mg calcium

p.28/29 Topped Bruschetta: with Roasted Vegetable Topping
363Kcals; 4g protein; 29g total fat; 4g saturated fat; 24g carbohydrate; 1g fibre; 229mg sodium; 54mg calcium
with Duck Topping
350Kcals; 16.5g protein; 22g total fat; 3.5g saturated fat; 22g carbohydrate; 1g fibre; 287mg sodium; 60mg calcium

p.31 Crunchy Chicken Salad
400Kcals; 23g protein; 31g total fat; 5g saturated fat; 7g carbohydrate; 1g fibre; 324mg sodium; 37mg calcium

p.31 Chicken Stuffed Pittas
530Kcals; 29g protein; 18g total fat; 3g saturated fat; 66g carbohydrate; 4g fibre; 665mg sodium; 126mg calcium

p.32 Chinese Style Pork
204Kcals; 22g protein; 10g total fat; 2g saturated fat; 7g carbohydrate; 2.5g fibre; 424mg sodium; 45mg calcium

p.32 Spicy Beef
460Kcals; 37g protein; 29g total fat; 7.5g saturated fat; 7g carbohydrate; 1.5g fibre; 275mg sodium; 68mg calcium

p.33 Sausage & Bean Casserole
553Kcals; 22g protein; 45g total fat; 13g saturated fat; 15g carbohydrate; 4g fibre; 1961mg sodium; 53mg calcium

p.34 Seared Calf's Liver with Crispy Bacon
417Kcals; 27g protein; 34g total fat; 12g saturated fat; 2g carbohydrate; 0g fibre; 1019mg sodium; 11mg calcium

p.34 Lamb with Crispy Potatoes
319Kcals; 23g protein; 14g total fat; 5g saturated fat; 26g carbohydrate; 1.5g fibre; 84mg sodium; 30mg calcium

p.35 Bacon & Mushroom Omelette
377Kcals; 36g protein; 26g total fat; 7g saturated fat; 0.5g carbohydrate; 1.5g fibre; 1860mg sodium; 85mg calcium

p.36 Ratatouille Gratin
208Kcals; 5g protein; 12g total fat; 2g saturated fat; 21g carbohydrate; 4.5g fibre; 19mg sodium; 42mg calcium

p.37 Tabbouleh
270Kcals; 13g protein; 9g total fat; 2g saturated fat; 36g carbohydrate; 1.5g fibre; 535mg sodium; 43mg calcium

p.37 Spinach & Potato Curry
214Kcals; 8g protein; 7g total fat; 1g saturated fat; 31g carbohydrate; 6.5g fibre; 99mg sodium; 143mg calcium

p.38 Mushroom & Parma Ham Pizza
352Kcals; 14g protein; 17g total fat; 3g saturated fat; 38g carbohydrate; 3g fibre; 585mg sodium; 191mg calcium

p.38 Chunky Spanish Omelette
333Kcals; 16g protein; 22g total fat; 4.5g saturated fat; 19g carbohydrate; 4g fibre; 140mg sodium; 90mg calcium

p.42 Haddock with Beetroot
222Kcals; 31.5g protein; 7g total fat; 1g saturated fat; 10g carbohydrate; 2g fibre; 293mg sodium; 57mg calcium

p.42 Seared Tuna with Mixed Bean Salad
657Kcals; 62g protein; 29g total fat; 5g saturated fat; 38g carbohydrate; 13g fibre; 1050mg sodium; 186mg calcium

p.43 Warm Scallop & Avocado Salad
622Kcals; 34g protein; 51g total fat; 7g saturated fat; 7.5g carbohydrate; 4g fibre; 230mg sodium; 78mg calcium

p.44 Poached Salmon with Fresh Herb Dressing
330Kcals; 28g protein; 18g total fat;

3g saturated fat; 2.5g carbohydrate; 0.5g fibre; 157mg sodium; 58mg calcium

p.45 Roast Monkfish with Green Lentils
355Kcals; 45g protein; 5g total fat; 1g saturated fat; 36g carbohydrate; 8g fibre; 39mg sodium; 68mg calcium

p.45 Red Mullet with Gooseberries
543Kcals; 80g protein; 18g total fat; 0.5g saturated fat; 13.5g carbohydrate; 2.0g fibre; 367mg sodium; 294mg calcium

p.46 Paella
450Kcals; 34g protein; 10g total fat; 2g saturated fat; 55g carbohydrate; 2.5g fibre; 261mg sodium; 94mg calcium

p.46 Fennel-stuffed Sea Bass
372Kcals; 55g protein; 12g total fat; 2g saturated fat; 1g carbohydrate; 1g fibre; 234mg sodium; 444mg calcium

p.48 Turkey with Preserved Lemons & Couscous
610Kcals; 65g protein; 15g total fat; 2.5g saturated fat; 48g carbohydrate; 1.5g fibre; 175mg sodium; 58mg calcium

p.49 Coq au Vin
500Kcals; 39g protein; 32g total fat; 10g saturated fat; 4.5g carbohydrate; 1g fibre; 764mg sodium; 29mg calcium

p.50 Thai Green Curry
550Kcals; 42g protein; 39g total fat; 31g saturated fat; 8g carbohydrate; 0g fibre; 422mg sodium; 32mg calcium

p.50 Turkey Tikka
236Kcals; 49g protein; 7g total fat; 1g saturated fat; 2g carbohydrate; 0g fibre; 314mg sodium; 35mg calcium

p.51 Pheasant Pie
991Kcals; 48g protein; 52g total fat; 11g saturated fat; 87g carbohydrate; 9g fibre; 532mg sodium; 220mg calcium

p.53 Poussin with Sticky Glaze
560Kcals; 42g protein; 39g total fat; 10g saturated fat; 9g carbohydrate; 0.5g fibre; 153mg sodium; 25mg calcium

p.53 Duck with Cranberries
680Kcals; 35g protein; 53g total fat; 14g saturated fat; 16.5g carbohydrate; 2g fibre; 217mg sodium; 47mg calcium

p.54 Venison & Vegetable Pot Pies
330Kcals; 41g protein; 11g total fat; 3g saturated fat; 15.5g carbohydrate; 4g fibre; 140mg sodium; 66mg calcium

p.55 Chilli Beef Salad
280Kcals; 31g protein; 17g total fat; 4g saturated fat; 2.5g carbohydrate; 2g fibre; 86mg sodium; 75mg calcium

p.57 Lamb Tikka
813Kcals; 52g protein; 39g total fat; 20g saturated fat; 62g carbohydrate; 0g fibre; 277mg sodium; 57mg calcium

p.57 Roast Lamb with Shiitake
285Kcals; 32g protein; 17g total fat; 6.5g saturated fat; 2g carbohydrate; 0.5g fibre; 109mg sodium; 29mg calcium

p.58 Lamb & Apricot Cobbler
675Kcals; 45g protein; 31g total fat; 8g saturated fat; 57g carbohydrate; 7g fibre; 540mg sodium; 253mg calcium

p.59 Fruity Pork Casserole
366Kcals; 34g protein; 12g total fat; 3g saturated fat; 21g carbohydrate; 2.5g fibre; 127mg sodium; 49mg calcium

p.61 Vegetable Stir-fry
386Cal; 12g protein; 10g total fat; 1g saturated fat; 65g carbohydrate; 6.5g fibre; 369mg sodium; 58mg calcium

p.64 Curried Sweet Potato
165Kcals; 1.5g protein; 8g total fat; 1g saturated fat; 24g carbohydrate; 3g fibre; 45mg sodium; 27mg calcium

p.65 Seared New Potatoes with Rosemary & Sea Salt
256–170Kcals; 4–2.5g protein; 12–8g total fat; 2–1g saturated fat; 36–24g carbohydrate; 2.5–1.5g fibre; 510–340mg sodium; 14–9mg calcium

p.65 Potato Cakes
205Kcals; 6g protein; 8g total fat; 1g saturated fat; 30g carbohydrate; 2.5g fibre; 75mg sodium; 31mg calcium

p.66 Perfect Jacket Potatoes
183Kcals; 4g protein; 6g total fat; 1g saturated fat; 31g carbohydrate; 2.5g fibre; 13mg sodium; 10mg calcium

p.68 Courgettes with Bell Pepper, Garlic & Rosemary
106Kcals; 4.5g protein; 6.5g total fat; 1g saturated fat; 7g carbohydrate; 3g fibre; 4mg sodium; 60mg calcium

p.68 Orange-glazed Baby Carrots
45Kcals; 1g protein; 0.6g total fat; 0.1g saturated fat; 9g carbohydrate; 3g fibre; 52mg sodium; 45mg calcium

p.69 Pumpkin with Caraway Seeds
205Kcals; 1.5g protein; 17.5g total fat; 1g saturated fat; 10.5g carbohydrate; 2g fibre; 175mg sodium; 61mg calcium

p.69 Patty Pan Risotto
378Kcals; 8.5g protein; 6.5g total fat; 1g saturated fat; 73g carbohydrate; 1g fibre; 2mg sodium; 59mg calcium

p.70 Mediterranean Stuffed Aubergine
70Kcals; 2.5g protein; 4g total fat; 1g saturated fat; 7.5g carbohydrate; 5g fibre; 11mg sodium; 33mg calcium

p.71 Gnocchi-topped Vegetables
470Kcals; 15g protein; 14g total fat; 2.5g saturated fat; 76g carbohydrate; 7g fibre; 1119mg sodium; 120mg calcium

p.72 Fennel & Mangetout Stir-fry
105Kcals; 4g protein; 8g total fat; 1.5g saturated fat; 4.5g carbohydrate; 2g fibre; 980mg sodium; 31mg calcium

p.72 Vegetarian Stuffed Cabbage
180Kcals; 6g protein; 13g total fat; 1g saturated fat; 10.5g carbohydrate; 6g fibre; 10mg sodium; 101mg calcium

p.73 Red Cabbage with Pears
145Kcals; 2.5g protein; 3g total fat; 0.5g saturated fat; 29g carbohydrate; 4.5g fibre; 13mg sodium; 80mg calcium

p.75 Roast Tomatoes with Balsamic Vinegar
150Kcals; 2g protein; 11.5g total fat; 2g saturated fat; 11g carbohydrate; 2.5g fibre; 19mg sodium; 20mg calcium

p.75 Triple Tomato & Avocado Salad
242Kcals; 2g protein; 22.5g total fat; 4g saturated fat; 8g carbohydrate; 3g fibre; 11mg sodium; 16mg calcium

p.76 Basic White Sauce
435Kcals; 13g protein; 29g total fat; 1.5g saturated fat; 31.5g carbohydrate; 0g fibre; 360mg sodium; 64mg calcium

p.76 Mayonnaise
(per 15ml) 80Kcals; 0.5g protein; 9g total fat; 1.2g saturated fat; 0g carbohydrate; 0g fibre; 6.3mg sodium; 2.5mg calcium

p.77 Tomato Sauce
590Kcals; 12g protein; 37g total fat; 16g saturated fat; 54g carbohydrate; 16g fibre; 209mg sodium; 132mg calcium

p.80 Avocado & Tuna Stuffed Tomato
360Kcals; 21g protein; 21.5g total fat; 4g saturated fat; 22g carbohydrate; 6g fibre; 368mg sodium; 48mg calcium

p.81 Tomato Catherine Wheels
13Kcals; 0.6g protein; 0.2g total fat; 0g saturated fat; 2g carbohydrate; 0.2g fibre; 13mg sodium; 3mg calcium

p.83 Fish Cakes with Salsa
195Kcals; 15g protein; 6g total fat; 1g saturated fat; 22g carbohydrate; 2g fibre; 198mg sodium; 44mg calcium

p.84 Chicken Goujons & Chips
490Kcals; 22g protein; 33.5g total fat; 5g saturated fat; 26.5g carbohydrate; 1g fibre; 129mg sodium; 27mg calcium

p.85 Beef Meatballs with Gooey Centres
466Kcals; 39g protein; 30g total fat; 10g saturated fat; 11g carbohydrate; 2g fibre; 441mg sodium; 73mg calcium

p.85 Polenta-topped Pie
460Kcals; 41g protein; 20g total fat; 8g saturated fat; 28g carbohydrate; 2g fibre; 263mg sodium; 37mg calcium

p.86 Spaghetti Carbonara
415Kcals; 25g protein; 12g total fat; 3g saturated fat; 54g carbohydrate; 2.5g fibre; 1193mg sodium; 43mg calcium

p.86 Ham & Egg Parcels
176Kcals; 12g protein; 4g total fat; 1g saturated fat; 20g carbohydrate; 0.5g fibre; 402mg sodium; 11mg calcium

p.88 Pork & Apple Burgers
330Kcals; 19g protein; 6g total fat; 1.5g saturated fat; 52g carbohydrate; 2g fibre; 557mg sodium; 119mg calcium

p.89 Pizza with Pork & Sweetcorn
340Kcals; 15.5g protein; 20g total fat; 5.5g saturated fat; 25g carbohydrate; 2.5g fibre; 458mg sodium; 151mg calcium

p.89 Honey Sausages & Mash
527Kcals; 13g protein; 27g total fat; 9.5g saturated fat; 62g carbohydrate; 3g fibre; 725mg sodium; 56mg calcium

p.90 Baked Marmalade Steamed Puddings
686Kcals; 9.5g protein; 35g total fat; 9g saturated fat; 86g carbohydrate; 1g fibre; 362mg sodium; 176mg calcium

p.91 Chocolate Bread Pudding
405Kcals; 7g protein; 20g total fat; 6.5g saturated fat; 51.5g carbohydrate; 1g fibre; 301mg sodium; 70mg calcium

p.91 Flapjacks
245Kcals; 3.5g protein; 13g total fat; 3g saturated fat; 30.5g carbohydrate; 2g fibre; 101mg sodium; 25mg calcium

p.93 Mini Plum Crumbles
335Kcals; 3.5g protein; 11g total fat; 3g saturated fat; 60g carbohydrate; 2.5g fibre; 113mg sodium; 66mg calcium

p.93 Fruity Milk Shakes
220Kcals; 12g protein; 8g total fat; 1.5g saturated fat; 27g carbohydrate; 3g fibre; 46mg sodium; 48mg calcium

p.93 Chocolate Chip Muffins
100Kcals; 1g protein; 6.5g total fat; 2g saturated fat; 10g carbohydrate; 0.5g fibre; 89mg sodium; 27mg calcium

p.96 Bluebery Rice Pudding
528Kcals; 2g protein; 41g total fat; 32g saturated fat; 19g carbohydrate; 1g fibre; 34mg sodium; 45mg calcium

p.97 Baked Chocolate Puddings with Chocolate Sauce
637Kcals; 11g protein; 33g total fat; 14g saturated fat; 80g carbohydrate; 2g fibre; 322mg sodium; 69mg calcium

p.97 Baked Mini Pineapples
326Kcals; 4g protein; 0.5g total fat; 0.1g saturated fat; 80g carbohydrate; 4.5g fibre; 55mg sodium; 58mg calcium

p.98 Hot Fruit Soufflé with Sloe Gin-Macerated Fruits
300Kcals; 6g protein; 8.5g total fat; 2.5g saturated fat; 49g carbohydrate; 1.5g fibre; 155mg sodium; 52mg calcium

p.98 Hot Coffee Soufflé
210Kcals; 9g protein; 12g total fat; 3.5g saturated fat; 16g carbohydrate; 1g fibre; 145mg sodium; 44mg calcium

p.99 Souffléed Omelette with Caramelized Orchard Fruits
350Kcals; 12.5g protein; 10g total fat; 3g saturated fat; 59g carbohydrate; 6g fibre; 141mg sodium; 78mg calcium

p.99 Blueberry Clafoutis
235Kcals; 11g protein; 10.5g total fat; 3g saturated fat; 26g carbohydrate; 1g fibre; 131mg sodium; 76mg calcium

p.101 Crème Brûlée
200Kcals; 5g protein; 3.5g total fat; 0.5g saturated fat; 40g carbohydrate; 1g fibre; 1mg sodium; 10mg calcium

p.101 Toffee Bananas
365Kcals; 2g protein; 15g total fat; 2g saturated fat; 56g carbohydrate; 1g fibre; 26mg sodium; 47mg calcium

p.102 Warm Spiced Fruit Compote
228Kcals; 2.5g protein; 0.5g total fat; 0.1g saturated fat; 50g carbohydrate; 7g fibre; 20mg sodium; 42mg calcium

p.102 Poached Pears
227Kcals; 0.5g protein; 0.2g total fat; 0g saturated fat; 49g carbohydrate; 3.5g fibre; 12mg sodium; 25mg calcium

p.103 Fresh Fruit Terrine
90–68Kcals; 6–4.5g protein; 0.5–0.4g total fat; 0.2–0.1g saturated fat; 17–12.5g carbohydrate; 4–3g fibre; 28–21mg sodium; 59–45mg calcium

p.103 Upside-down Fruit Tart
427Kcals; 6.5g protein; 16g total fat; 3.5g saturated fat; 68g carbohydrate; 1g fibre; 270mg sodium; 138mg calcium

p.104 Individual Summer Puddings
253Kcals; 6g protein; 1g total fat; 0.2g saturated fat; 58g carbohydrate; 2.5g fibre; 290mg sodium; 84mg calcium

p.104 Orchard Strudel
223Kcals; 3g protein; 0.6g total fat; 0g saturated fat; 54g carbohydrate; 3g fibre; 3mg sodium; 12mg calcium

p.107 Raspberry Ice Meringue Nest
228Kcals; 6g protein; 4.5g total fat; 1g saturated fat; 44g carbohydrate; 1g fibre; 41mg sodium; 25mg calcium

p.108 Mango Sorbet
56Kcals; 1.5g protein; 0g total fat; 0g saturated fat; 13.5g carbohydrate; 0.5g fibre; 25mg sodium; 10mg calcium

p.108 Strawberry Granita
102Kcals; 0.7g protein; 0g total fat; 0g saturated fat; 12g carbohydrate; 1g fibre; 14mg sodium; 21mg calcium

p.109 Coconut Ice Cream with Curried Fruit Salad
500Kcals; 6g protein; 31g total fat; 22g saturated fat; 37g carbohydrate; 2g fibre; 60mg sodium; 47mg calcium

p.112 Chestnut Log
251Kcals; 7g protein; 7.5g total fat; 3g saturated fat; 41g carbohydrate; 0.5g fibre; 45mg sodium; 42mg calcium

p.112 Spicy Syrup Cake
485Kcals; 7g protein; 21g total fat; 6g saturated fat; 72g carbohydrate; 1.5g fibre; 372mg sodium; 183mg calcium

p.113 Carrot Cake
270Kcals; 7g protein; 3g total fat; 1g saturated fat; 58g carbohydrate; 2g fibre; 239mg sodium; 169mg calcium

p.115 Chocolate Cake Bars
210Kcals; 3.5g protein; 10.5g total fat; 2g saturated fat; 27g carbohydrate; 1g fibre; 126mg sodium; 84mg calcium

p.115 Mocha Bars
160Kcals; 3g protein; 3.5g total fat; 1.5g saturated fat; 31g carbohydrate; 1g fibre; 27mg sodium; 25mg calcium

p.116 Simple Fruit Cake
600Kcals; 7g protein; 21g total fat; 6g saturated fat; 104g carbohydrate; 2.5g fibre; 356mg sodium; 155mg calcium

p.116 Strawberry & Cardamom Roll
170Kcals; 6.5g protein; 4.5g total fat; 1g saturated fat; 28g carbohydrate; 0.5g fibre; 44mg sodium; 40mg calcium

p.117 Fresh Fruit Tartlets
50Kcals; 1.5g protein; 0.5g total fat; 0.1g saturated fat; 10g carbohydrate; 0.8g fibre; 2mg sodium; 8mg calcium

p.117 Marzipan Baklava
218Kcals; 4.5g protein; 6g total fat; 0.5g saturated fat; 37.5g carbohydrate; 1.5g fibre; 5mg sodium; 25 mg calcium

p.118 Cinnamon Swirl Tea Ring
(whole loaf) 2975Kcals; 70g protein; 30g total fat; 5g saturated fat; 649g carbohydrate; 23g fibre; 6196mg sodium; 1037mg calcium

p.119 Citrus Rings with Summer Berries
592Kcals; 16g protein; 5g total fat; 1g saturated fat; 130g carbohydrate; 4g fibre; 1023mg sodium; 185mg calcium

p.119 Peanut Butter Cookies
92Kcals; 2.5g protein; 4g total fat; 1g saturated fat; 12g carbohydrate; 0.5g fibre; 50mg sodium; 25mg calcium

p.120 Savoury Tomato Scones
105Kcals; 4g protein; 2g total fat; 0.5g saturated fat; 19.5g carbohydrate; 1g fibre; 107mg sodium; 94mg calcium

p.120 Apricot Scones
105Kcals; 3.5g protein; 2g total fat; 0.5g saturated fat; 20g carbohydrate; 1g fibre; 75mg sodium; 70mg calcium

p.122 Focaccia
(whole loaf) 2048Kcals; 46g protein; 61g total fat; 8.5g saturated fat; 350g carbohydrate; 14g fibre; 5914mg sodium; 640mg calcium

p.123 Herb Bread Rolls
129Kcals; 4g protein; 0.5g total fat; 0.1g saturated fat; 29g carbohydrate; 1g fibre; 165mg sodium; 53mg calcium

p.123 Malt Loaf
(whole loaf) 1802Kcals; 49g protein; 27.5g total fat; 5g saturated fat; 363g carbohydrate; 26g fibre; 1116 mg sodium; 396mg calcium

Index

ACKNOWLEDGEMENTS

Food preparation: Lucy Knox
and Sarah Lowman
Art Director: Chrissie Lloyd
Nutritional analysis: Fiona
Hunter

Thanks also to Laura Price,
Sandra Brooke, Dawn
Henderson and Charlotte Beech
for their assistance.